A TASTE OF LATIN AMERICA

CULINARY TRADITIONS *and* CLASSIC RECIPES *from*
Argentina, Brazil, Chile, Colombia, Costa Rica, Cuba, Mexico, Peru, Puerto Rico & Venezuela

PATRICIA CARTIN

To my daughters, who have always been by my side in my
passion for the culinary arts —PC

An Imagine Book
Published by Charlesbridge
85 Main Street
Watertown, MA 02472
(617) 926-0329
www.imaginebooks.net

Library of Congress Cataloging-in-Publication Data
Names: Cartin, Patricia, author.
Title: A taste of Latin America : culinary traditions and classic recipes from Argentina, Brazil,
  Chile, Colombia, Costa Rica, Cuba, Mexico, Peru, Puerto Rico & Venezuela /
  by Patricia Cartin
Description: Watertown, MA : Charlesbridge, [2017] | "An Imagine Book." |
  Includes index.
Identifiers: LCCN 2017000105 (print) | LCCN 2017000891 (ebook) | ISBN
  9781623545215 (reinforced for library use) | ISBN 9781632892065 (ebook) |
  ISBN 9781632892072 (ebook pdf)
Subjects: LCSH: Cooking, Latin American. | LCGFT: Cookbooks.
Classification: LCC TX716.A1 C3925 2017 (print) | LCC TX716.A1 (ebook) | DDC
  641.598--dc23
LC record available at https://lccn.loc.gov/2017000105

Printed in China
(hc) 10 9 8 7 6 5 4 3 2 1

Designed by Joshua Seong
Production by Karen Matsu Greenberg
Illustrations by Katie Klasmeier

A TASTE OF LATIN AMERICA

CULINARY TRADITIONS *and* CLASSIC RECIPES *from*

Argentina, Brazil, Chile, Colombia, Costa Rica, Cuba, Mexico, Peru, Puerto Rico & Venezuela

PATRICIA CARTIN

imagine!

CONTENTS

5

IN
TRO
DUC
TION

MEXICO

CUBA

PUERTO RICO

COSTA RICA

COLOMBIA

VENEZUELA

PERU

BRAZIL

CHILE

ARGENTINA

It is easy to view Latin America as one homogenous block of nations. All, with the exception of Brazil, speak Spanish. Nearly all were conquered during one of Christopher Columbus's explorations of the New World. All have benefitted from the influences of immigrants from other nations. Yet each Latin American country is distinct in its own right—particularly where its unique flavors of food is concerned.

The West Indies islands of Cuba and Puerto Rico are both surrounded by the Caribbean Sea. They are both tropical. Yet, their meals contrast greatly. While Cuban food is generally mild, relying on its omnipresent "mojo" sauce for its unique flavor, Puerto Rican food can be wildly spicy. Cuba's culinary roots reflect both its African and Spanish heritage; its Haitian influence as much as the French who colonized Haiti. Puerto Rico's cuisine also demonstrates African and Spanish origins, with the American influence being undeniable.

Mexican cuisine is likely most familiar to our palettes in the US, although its true variety is often lost on Americans who view it as little more than "fast food." In truth, this Latin American nation offers a fusion of foods from cultures thousands of years old. The Mayans and Aztecs not only cultivated the corn now essential to so many Mexican dishes, they also harvested chocolate, chili peppers, and wonderfully exotic at the time delicacies like the avocado. All of these ingredients remain modern staples.

Despite its small size, Central America's Costa Rica enjoys an amazing diversity of climates ranging from rainforests to mountain ranges. Its northern Caribbean coast is one of the world's largest producers of bananas. Nearer the middle of the country, sugarcane and coffee plants spread to nearly every empty plot, no matter how small. Along the Pacific Coast, one's menu depends upon the abundance of the sea. There are simply no generalities when it comes to Costa Rican cooking.

Perhaps it is South America that holds the most surprises. Fourth in size after North America, this continent is one of geographic extremes. While Venezuelan coastal cities regularly deal with temperatures in the hundreds, its mountain peaks are sub-zero year round. Here, fresh produce is always in season and the Italian influence is obvious in Venezuela's "Latin Americanized" versions of lasagne and other pasta dishes.

Colombian meals are hearty affairs, relying heavily on beef, pork, and seafood. Soups and stews are particular favorites, regardless of the weather forecast. Spanish mainstays like rice and beans are go-to meals, while coffee and chocolate beverages are enjoyed from morning to evening.

Brazil was not colonized by Spain but rather Portugal. Like the US, it has a substantial immigrant population comprised of Germans, Japanese, Middle Easterners, and others. The cuisine is a broad, bold representation of all of these cultures. To Brazil's south lies Argentina. Like Brazil, Argentina's acceptance of settlers from other lands adds to its cuisine's diversity. But, Argentina places a uniquely delicious focus on beef. The centuries-old gaucho tradition of open-air barbecuing is alive and well, as evidenced by the fact that Argentines consume twice as much beef per person per year than North Americans. But don't be mislead into thinking this is a one-ingredient nation. The ocean provides a bountiful selection of seafood like salmon and shellfish, and its fertile vineyards produce some of the world's finest wines. Desserts are expected, not neglected in Argentina—many of them served with the silky, sweet sauce known as Dulce le Leche.

Peru, once the home of the Incas, mastered agricultural techniques several millennia before other civilizations. The ancestors of nearly all potatoes cultivated worldwide were born here, as were lima beans, sweet potatoes, maize, squashes, and other produce. Like Mexicans—whose chili peppers Peru's farmers adopted and cross-pollinated with their own native species—Peruvians prefer their food both spicy and citrusy. Ceviche, literally "cooking" fish in the acid of lemon or lime juice, is a flagship of Peruvian cuisine. A large Chinese population in Peru has popularized "chifa." Although these menu items are prepared using traditional Asian cooking methods, typical Asian ingredients are scarce in Peru. They are therefore swapped out for indigenous selections. The result is a delicious integration of two powerful flavor profiles. Chile is a ribbon of land on South America's Pacific Coast. While the sea yields a multitude of edible delicacies, the significant German population introduced the pork dishes and pastry desserts that have become synonymous with the Chilean culinary scene. The foods of the indigenous peoples are still cooked and served much like they were in that bygone era. Every bit of an ear of corn is utilized, from its kernels to its husk, and beans appear in nearly every hearty bowl of seafood stew or vegetable soup.

A Taste of Latin America is not only a cookbook—although the recipes are flavorsome examples of what make this region's cuisine incomparable. It is also a journey through the history and daily lives of the people of Latin America. Come along and experience this world as few ever will. Buen provecho!

ARGENTINA

Argentina sits on the southern tail of South America. The Atlantic Ocean forms its eastern border, while Chile serves as a thin boundary between its western edge and the Pacific Ocean.

The influence of its indigenous peoples combined with the customs of the later arriving Europeans has made Argentina's cuisine one of the most diverse in the world. Second only to the United States in immigrant population, Argentina's melting pot includes Italians, British, and Germans to name only a few. Each culture has created its own distinct approach to the country's Latin American cuisine.

Argentines consume nearly 100 pounds of beef per person per year—twice as much as Americans. The nation is synonymous with asado—a method of slow-cooking meat over an open fire made famous by Argentina's gauchos (cowboys). There are no marinades and smoke is kept to a minimum by diverting the grease drippings away from the flames. Nothing is meant to detract from the flavor of the beef itself.

Of course, Argentines eat more than just red meat. In the southern region, the Atlantic Ocean provides an abundant supply of salmon, squid, and shellfish. This is also where most of the nation's chocolate is produced, and where many German immigrants reside.

Cooks in northeast Argentina turn simple cornbread into a decadent main course. Sopa paraguaya, a traditional Paraguayan and Northern Argentine food, combines cottage and other cheeses, fresh corn kernels, sautéed onions, and egg into a rich, moist delicacy. Argentina's national beverage, yerba mate, is brewed from the dried leaves and twigs of the holly trees growing in this region. This hot, bitter tea is consumed communally, all persons drinking from the same gourd.

The cuisine in Argentina's northwest region bears a resemblance to that of Mexico, while the central plains around Buenos Aires offer a wonderful variety of Latin Americanized Italian dishes. Sorrentinos are oversized ravioli stuffed with ham and cheese. Pizza dough is often made from flour ground from garbanzo beans. Pizzas are typically double-crusted, the middle stuffing made from whatever ingredients the pizza-maker has on hand.

Regardless of your dessert choice, it will likely include dulce de leche, a thick sweet sauce that works as well as a pastry filling as it does in a coffee beverage. And, speaking of beverages, though Argentina's wine production dates back hundreds of years, the industry is experiencing a renaissance. Fine examples of these wines are now found readily in America.

Whether you start with the empanadas or decide to try your hand at the spicy choripán sandwiches, these recipes are sure to bring out the gaucho spirit in you.

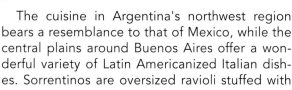

MEDIALUNAS [MEH-dee-ah-LOOH-nahs]

Croissants

Medialunas are the Argentine's variation of croissants - delicious for breakfast or with afternoon coffee.

INGREDIENTS

Butter Paste

¼ cup flour

4 sticks of butter, sliced in 1-inch thick pieces

For the rolls:

¾ cup warm milk

1 tsp. salt

3 tsp. active dry yeast

4 cups flour, plus more if needed

¼ cup sugar

2 eggs

1 tsp. honey

1 tsp. vanilla

1 tsp. orange or lemon zest

For the eggwash:

1 egg

1 tbsp. milk

For the glaze:

1 cup water

1 cup sugar

1 tbsp. rum or orange liquor

DIRECTIONS

Preheat oven to 400° F.

1. In a small bowl add warm milk, 1 tsp. sugar and 3 tsp of yeast, let sit to dissolve until the yeast is foamy.

2. In a large bowl combine 4 cups flour, salt, and the rest of the sugar. Toss the dry ingredients and make a hole in the center. Add 2 eggs, honey, vanilla, zest, and warm milk-yeast mixture to the hole. Combine with a fork, then knead the dough with your hands. Make a ball and let the dough rest for 30 minutes (covered) in an oiled bowl.

3. On a floured surface, roll out the dough, making a 1/4" thick rectangle (18 x 10). Make the butter paste and add it to the center. Begin folding the edges from left to center, then from right to center to form a square, then fold the edges over again, like a book. Wrap the dough in plastic and refrigerate 20 minutes.

4. Remove the dough from the refrigerator and place again on a floured surface. Roll out again to make a 25 x 14 inch rectangle. Folding as direction above and repeat the process rolling, folding and refrigerating, 4 times in total.

5. Then cut in half lengthwise to make two long, narrow rectangles. Now cut each of these rectangles into small triangles, each with about 3 inches at their base. Each rectangle yields 12-15 triangles.

6. Roll each triangle from the base to the tip, then press a little until the tip is under the roll. Pull the two ends together to form a crescent shape and place them on a parchment paper lined-baking sheet and let rise in a warm place for 30 minutes.

7. Lightly beat the remaining egg with a fork and add 1 tbsp. milk to create an egg wash. Brush rolls with wash. Bake for 20 to 25 minutes or until golden.

8. While the rolls are baking, make the glaze. Boil water with sugar until sugar is dissolved and liquid thickens, then add rum. Set aside.

9. When medialunas are cold, brush them with the glaze and serve.

TIP

Delicious served with coffee for breakfast or brunch.

TOTAL TIME:
4 HOURS
DIFFICULTY:
ADVANCED
PORTIONS:
24 TO 30

CHIMICHURRI [CHI-mee-CHOO-ree]

Green sauce

An Argentinian "pesto" of sorts, chimichurri is a delicious green sauce made with fresh herbs, typically used as a marinade or an accompaniment to all cuts of beef.

INGREDIENTS

- ½ cup fresh cilantro, finely chopped
- ½ cup fresh parsley, finely chopped
- ¼ cup fresh oregano, finely chopped
- 3 garlic cloves, minced
- 3 tbs. fresh lemon juice
- 1 tbs. white vinegar
- ¼ cup red wine vinegar
- ½ cup extra virgin olive oil
- 1 tsp. crushed red pepper flakes (optional)

DIRECTIONS

1. In a medium bowl, toss the chopped herbs with the minced garlic.

2. Stir in lemon juice and vinegars; then slowly drizzle in the olive oil.

3. Set aside at least 2 hours. Serve at room temperature.

CHORIPÁN [chor-ee-PAN]

Sandwich with chorizo sausage

"Chori" is short for "chorizo," a spicy sausage. "Pan" is "bread" in Spanish. Choripánes are delicious sandwiches that use chimichurri sauce as an integral part of the experience.

INGREDIENTS

- 1 pound Argentinian chorizo, sliced lengthwise
- 1 baguette or 2-3 hot dog buns
- 2 tbsp. soft butter

   Chimichurri sauce

DIRECTIONS

1. Heat grill to medium.

2. Place the chorizo on grill until fully cooked, about 8-10 minutes per side. Remove from grill and set aside.

3. Slice the bread lengthwise, spread butter on each half. Place halves in the grill, inside down. Toast and remove from grill.

4. Spread insides of bread with chimichurri sauce.

5. Sandwich the chorizo between two slices of the warm bread.

TOTAL TIME:
15 MINUTES
DIFFICULTY:
EASY
PORTIONS:
8-10 SERVINGS

TOTAL TIME:
20-25 MINUTES
DIFFICULTY:
EASY
PORTIONS:
2-3 SANDWICHES

LOCRO [LOH-kroh]

Stew of meat and vegetables

This deliciously creamy, thick stew is especially popular in the Andes region.

INGREDIENTS

- 2 cups dried, broken hominy
- 1 cup dried lima beans
- 1 cup dried chickpeas
- 1 pound beef short ribs with bone, cut in pieces
- 1 pound pork ribs with bone, cut in pieces
- ½ pound chorizo, cut in pieces
- 3 bay leaves
- ½ tsp. ground cumin
- 1 tsp. paprika
- 1 tsp. dried oregano
- 5 garlic cloves
- 1 onion
- Salt
- Pepper
- 1 fresh lemon juice
- 1 pound butternut squash, peeled and roughly chopped
- 4 carrots, peeled and roughly chopped
- 1 potato, peeled and roughly chopped
- 2 ears of corn

DIRECTIONS

1. Place hominy, lima beans, and chickpeas in a large, deep pot. Cover with water. Leave to soak overnight. Drain the beans before using.

2. In a large dutch oven, add the meats, hominy, chickpeas, and lima beans, and add water to cover. Stir in bay leaves, cumin, paprika, dry oregano, onion, and garlic, and bring to a boil.

3. Reduce heat and simmer, partially covered, for 4 hours, stirring occasionally.

4. Add salt, pepper, and vegetables, and simmer an additional hour or so, until vegetables are tender.

5. Spoon out stew into individual bowls. Serve warm.

TIP

For Vegetarian Locro

In step 2, omit the meat, add 3 cups vegetable broth and enough water to cover.

When step 4 is complete, spoon soup ingredients into a blender, mix all soup ingredients until smooth (remove kernels from cob before blending). Add ½ cream for flavor and consistency. Bring to a boil and serve. Garnish with scallions.

TOTAL TIME:
6 HOURS
(plus overnight soak
for beans)
DIFFICULTY:
EASY
PORTIONS:
12 SERVINGS

EMPANADAS [Ehm-pah-NAH-thahs]

Meat patties

Argentine empanadas are typically known for their meat filling and can either be fried or baked. You can also stuff the pastry with vegetables, such as spinach and mushroom, spinach and hard boiled egg, or with capresse (tomato, cheese and basil).

INGREDIENTS

For the Pastry Dough:

- 2 cups boiling water
- 1 stick butter
- 1 tsp. salt
- 3 cups flour, sifted
- 2 egg yolks (for egg wash)
-    Granulated sugar (optional)

For the Filling:

- 3 tbsp. butter or olive oil
- 1 onion, finely chopped
- 3 garlic cloves, finely chopped
- 1 tsp. sweet paprika
- 1 tsp. hot paprika
- 1 pound ground beef
- 4 ounces chorizo
- ¼ cup vegetable broth
- ½ cup raisins
- ¼ cup green olives pitted, chopped
- 1 tsp. ground cumin
- 1 tsp. dry oregano
- 1 tsp. ground thyme
- ½ tsp. salt
- ½ tsp. pepper
-    Extra oil, for frying

DIRECTIONS

Make the Dough:

1. In a large bowl add 2 cups boiling water, butter, and salt. Stir to dissolve and set aside to cool.

2. When the water mixture cools to room temperature, gradually stir in flour. Work with wooden spoon until dough comes together. If the dough is very sticky, add a pinch more flour and stir.

3. Remove the dough from the bowl and place on a lightly floured surface. Knead the dough for approximately 6-8 minutes and form into a ball. Wrap in plastic wrap and refrigerate 30 minutes.

Make the Filling:

1. Heat olive oil or butter in a large frying pan. Add onion and garlic and sauté for about 5 to 7 minutes, until softened. Stir in sweet paprika and hot paprika.

2. Add ground beef and chorizo and toss ingredients well. Brown for about 8-10 minutes.

3. Add vegetable broth and bring to a boil. Reduce heat to low.

4. Add raisins, olives, ground cumin, ground oregano, thyme, salt and pepper and simmer an additional 10 minutes, until liquid reduces. Set aside to cool.

Make the Empanadas:

1. Preheat oven to 350° F.

2. Remove dough from refrigerator and roll out over a floured surface.

3. Cut dough into 5-inch rounds. Fill each round with approximately a teaspoon of the meat mixture, being careful not to overfill. Touch the edges of the pastry with water on your fingertips; then fold over in a half-moon. Press the edges together with the tines of a fork.

4. Place the empanadas on a baking sheet and brush with egg yolk. Sprinkle with granulated sugar, if desired.

5. Bake at 350° F for about 15-18 minutes, or until golden. Serve warm or at room temperature.

TIP

Wrap and pack for lunch.

TOTAL TIME:
1½ HOURS
DIFFICULTY:
INTERMEDIATE
PORTIONS:
12-15 EMPANADAS

HUMITAS   [hoo-MEE-tahs]

Fresh corn dough wrapped in corn husks

Humitas are like tamales, though these are made with fresh corn husks whereas tamales are generally made with dried corn husks.

INGREDIENTS

12	ears of fresh corn with husks
1	tbsp. olive oil
2	medium white onions, finely chopped
½	tsp. dried crushed red pepper flakes
3	garlic cloves, minced
1	tsp. ground paprika
	Salt and pepper
1	tsp. ground cumin
½	cup heavy cream
¼	cup goat cheese

DIRECTIONS

1. Cut around the base of each ear of corn and gently remove husks, taking care to keep them fully intact. Place husks in a pot of boiling water 2-3 minutes. Drain and set aside.

2. With a knife, remove the kernels from each cob. Place corn kernels in a food processor and puree until roughly chopped. Set aside.

3. Warm the olive oil in a skillet over medium heat. Add the onions, red pepper flakes, and garlic, and sauté until soft – approximately 8-10 minutes.

4. Mix in the paprika, salt, pepper, and ground cumin. Next, add the pureed corn and toss well.

5. Add heavy cream and goat cheese and stir until cheese melts. Set aside to cool.

6. To assemble humitas, overlap 2 husks in an + shape. Now spoon corn mixture into the center. To close the wrap, fold the left side over the mixture, then fold the right side, then fold the top half and then the bottom half. Use the strips of the smaller husks or twine to tie around the wrap and secure.

7. Arrange the remaining husk parts in the bottom of a large deep pot. Place the humitas over the husks then add 2 cups of boiling water. Place on stove and let set 30 minutes. Serve warm.

TIP

Many cultures wrap corn kernels, corn mush or corn meal with vegetables and/or meat in some sort of leaf, and steam to cook. Humitas use corn husk to flavor the internal ingredients. Twine may also be used to tie around the wrapped husks.

TOTAL TIME:
1 HOUR
DIFFICULTY:
INTERMEDIATE
PORTIONS:
ABOUT 12-15

ALFAJORES [Al-Fah-HOR-Ehs]

Sugar cookie sandwich

Simple sandwich cookies filled with dulce de leche and covered with powdered sugar and coconut, alfajores are popular sweets from Argentina that are enjoyed throughout the world.

INGREDIENTS

1   cup cornstarch

¾   cup all-purpose flour, plus more as needed

1   tsp. baking powder

½   tsp. baking soda

    Pinch of salt

1   stick unsalted butter at room temperature

1/3   cup granulated sugar

3   egg yolks

½   tsp. vanilla extract

½   tsp. lemon zest

½   tsp. lemon extract

1   tsp. brandy

1   cup dulce de leche, at room temperature (see p. 68)

½   cup unsweetened coconut, shredded

    Powdered sugar, for dusting

DIRECTIONS

1. Preheat oven to 350° F. Line baking sheets with parchment paper.

2. Sift cornstarch, flour, baking powder, baking soda, and salt into a bowl and set aside.

3. In a separate large bowl, beat the butter and sugar together with an electric hand mixer or stand mixer with a paddle attachment until light and fluffy. Next, add egg yolks, one at a time, then add vanilla, lemon zest, lemon extract, and brandy.

4. Gradually fold in the dry ingredients with a spatula or use the low speed on your mixer. Press the mixture into a ball using your hands, then wrap ball in plastic wrap and place in refrigerator. Let sit 1 hour.

5. When the dough is chilled, roll it out on a lightly floured surface to a ¼-inch thickness. Using a round cookie cutter, cut dough into small rounds and place rounds over parchment paper on cookie sheet. Bake 8 to 10 minutes.

6. Remove from oven and place cookies on a wire rack to cool completely (approximately 30 minutes). When cooled, spread the undersides of half the rounds with 2 teaspoons of dulce de leche, then cover with another round. Roll the sides in the coconut and dust with powdered sugar.

TIP

Most Latin households have at least one jar of homemade Dulce de Leche (also called Manjar, or cream caramel), in their refrigerator. With its heavenly flavor, this edible "glue" holds the two cookie pieces together to create a perfect, delicate sandwich.

TOTAL TIME:
1½ HOURS
DIFFICULTY:
INTERMEDIATE
PORTIONS:
2 DOZEN
COOKIES

BRAZIL

At more than three million square miles, Brazil is the fifth largest nation in the world. Similar to the United States (the third largest country), Brazil's distinctly different climates and ethnic groups make for an incredibly diverse culinary experience.

Unlike other Latin American nations, Brazil was colonized not by Spain but by Portugal. Portuguese remains its national language. Brazil, however, is also a nation of immigrants. Some, such as the African slaves brought to work the sugar fields and gold mines, were forced to leave their homelands. Others, like Italians and Spaniards, came seeking one of the plentiful jobs in the coffee fields that, by the 1850s, were already producing half the world's yield.

As war-torn Europe became increasingly unstable in the late 19th and early 20th centuries, Germans flocked to South America. Middle Easterners came as well. After WWI, Japanese—for whom overpopulation in their homeland was becoming unbearable—emigrated to Brazil at a rate of 10,000 individuals per year. All of these newcomers influenced the nation's food and culture.

Brazil's indigenous ingredients include cassava, acai berries, Brazil nuts, and manioc root, from which the sauce tucupi is created. Europeans introduced wheat, dairy, and wine.

Southern Brazil borders Argentina and shares many of its gaucho traditions. In fact, the national dish, feijoada, is made of beef, black beans, bacon, and sausage. Sometimes cabbage, pumpkin, potatoes, or other vegetables are added. Traditionally, it is served with white rice and fresh orange slices.

Along the Atlantic Coast, particularly in the state of Bahia, African cuisine is predominant. Chili peppers and chili sauces seem to make their way into every meal. By contrast, in the Amazon Basin to the north, fish and tropical fruits such as papaya, mangos, and hog plums are staples.

Visitors from around the world flock to the Carnival of Brazil, an annual celebration held prior to the fasting season of lent. The Festa Junina, held in June, is Brazil's winter festival. Like the Carnival, there are costumes, dancing, and wonderful sweet treats like canjica, made with thickened coconut milk, fresh corn kernels, sugar, and cinnamon. The mixture is spilled out onto a platter to cool, then sliced and served as you would as pudding or porridge.

The recipes that follow capture the very essence of Brazilian cuisine. Cue the Samba mix, let the rhythm carry you to the kitchen, and treat your palette to one (or all) of these unique Latin American dishes.

FAROFA [Fahr-OH-Fa]

Fried cassava flour with eggs and bacon

Cassava flour (also called "yucca flour") toasted in butter is an essential side dish in many Brazilian homes.

INGREDIENTS

3-4 tbsp. butter

1 medium onion, finely diced

3 garlic cloves, minced

2 slices bacon

1½ cup cassava flour

1 handful parsley finely chopped

Salt and freshly ground black pepper

½ cup scallions, finely chopped

1 handful cilantro finely chopped

1 hardboiled egg, finely chopped (optional)

DIRECTIONS

1. Melt butter in a medium-sized skillet over medium-high heat. Sauté onions and garlic until they begin to brown—about 4-5 minutes.

2. Add bacon to the skillet and fry until browned.

3. Now add cassava flour and parsley and cook 7-8 minutes, stirring often, until golden brown.

4. Remove from heat. Season with salt and pepper. Fold in scallions and cilantro and add chopped hardboiled egg, if desired. Serve over feijoada (see p. 30) or rice.

TIP

Farofa may be prepared as a vegan dish by using ghee instead of butter and replacing the bacon and egg with 1/2 cup diced cashews.

TOTAL TIME:
30 MINUTES
DIFFICULTY:
EASY
PORTIONS:
4 SERVINGS

PAO DE QUEIJO   [Pow Duh KAY-zshoo]

Cheesy bread

A chewy and yummy treat that can be enjoyed as a snack at any time of day. If you want, you can prepare dough in advance and keep in the refrigerator for 3-4 days.

INGREDIENTS

- 1   cup whole milk
- ½   cup vegetable oil
- 1   stick butter
- 1   tsp. salt
- 2   cups cassava flour (or whole wheat flour if cassava flour not available)
- 2   eggs, lightly beaten
- 1   cup fresh shredded Parmesan cheese
- 1   cup shredded cheddar cheese

DIRECTIONS

1. Preheat the oven to 350° F. Line a baking sheet with parchment and set aside.

2. Combine the milk, oil, butter, and salt in a saucepan and bring to boil over medium heat. Remove from heat as soon as it starts to boil.

3. Stir the cassava flour to the mixture until the flour dissolves.

4. Now stir in the eggs and cheese and beat the dough for several minutes. Set dough aside to cool.

5. When dough is cooled, flour hands with cassava flour and shape into golf-sized balls and place on the parchment-lined baking sheet at least an inch and a half apart.

6. Bake for 25-30 minutes. Serve warm.

TIP

Don't expect these to stay around too long, and in fact, consider doubling the recipe so there are more than enough for dinner and lunch the next day.

FEIJOADA   [Fey-JUH-Wah-Duh]

Black bean chili

This authentic and delicious stew is a special treat for bean and meat lovers – with four different varieties of meat in the mix, it has depth and flavors that perfectly compliment black beans.

INGREDIENTS

18	oz. package sliced bacon
1	pound pork ribs (with bone)
3	chorizo or sausages
½	pound pork shoulder, cut into cubes
2	onions, chopped
4	garlic cloves, finely chopped
2	tbsp. olive oil
3	bay leaves
1	thyme string (fresh)
2	cups dried black beans, soaked overnight in cold water, then drained
	Salt and pepper, to taste

DIRECTIONS

1. Heat a large heavy saucepan, add the bacon and fry until crisp. Remove and keep the drippings in the pan. In batches sear the ribs, chorizo or sausages, and pork shoulder in the drippings.

2. Remove the meat and set aside. Now add the onion and garlic to the same saucepan. Sauté until soft—about 7-8 minutes.

3. Add the meats, bay leaves, thyme, and drained beans. Cover with water and bring to a boil, then reduce heat to a low simmer. Continue to cook for about 3 hours or until black beans are tender and meat falls off the bones.

4. Add salt and pepper to taste, and serve warm over white rice.

TIP

This meal is traditionally made for special events, holidays or celebrations. It is rich in flavors and perfect for large groups and is often served with farofa (see p. 26).

(Remember to add at least 2 hours to soak the beans, or soak them overnight.)

TOTAL TIME:
3½ TO 4 HOURS
DIFFICULTY:
INTERMEDIATE
PORTIONS:
4-6 SERVINGS

COXINHAS   [Koh-SHEEN-Yahs]

Fried cheese and chicken balls

These chicken croquettes are a popular and delicious street food in Brazil.

INGREDIENTS

- 2   skinless, boneless chicken breasts
- 4   cups chicken broth, plus more, as needed
- 1   onion, sliced in half
- 2-3   bay leaves
- 18   ounce package cream cheese
- 2   tsp. fresh lemon juice
- Salt, to taste
- 1   tbsp. olive oil
- 2   green onions, finely chopped
- 2   garlic cloves, finely chopped
- 2   eggs
- 3   cups breadcrumbs
- Vegetable oil, for frying

DIRECTIONS

1. In a large pot, add chicken breasts, chicken broth, onion, and bay leaves. If necessary, add water to completely cover chicken. Cook on medium heat for about 30 minutes, until chicken is tender.

2. When chicken is tender, remove from broth. Set aside to cool. Strain broth and set aside.

3. When cool, shred the chicken finely. Stir in cream cheese and lemon juice.

4. Heat olive oil in a large saucepan; sauté green onions and garlic. Stir in chicken mixture and mix well. Add salt to taste. Remove from heat and refrigerate.

5. Measure the remaining strained chicken broth and add more, if needed, to equal 3 cups. Pour broth into a large pot and heat to a boil. When boiling, add 3 cups flour and stir very vigorously while cooking for about 3 minutes, or until a stiff dough forms. Set aside to cool and once cool, refrigerate for 1 hour.

6. With floured hands, make the dough into balls about the size of golf balls. Use your fingertip to dig out the center; fill with chicken mixture and close the ball. Shape filled dough balls into drumsticks.

7. Whisk the eggs in a bowl. Add breadcrumbs to a different shallow bowl. Dip the coxinhas in the egg, then in the breadcrumbs. Chill for at least 1 hour before frying.

8. Heat vegetable oil in a heavy saucepan over medium-high heat. Fry the coxinhas in batches until golden brown. Drain on paper towels and serve warm.

TIP

When making these at home, you may serve them as a main course or a side dish.

TOTAL TIME:
3 HOURS
DIFFICULTY:
INTERMEDIATE
PORTIONS:
16 CROQUETTES

MOQUECA DE CAMARÃO [Moe-KET-cha Duh Ka-MAH-Ro]

Shrimp stew with coconut milk

A great comfort food or a way to dazzle guests – Moqueca de Camarão is an unforgettable fish and shrimp stew cooked in coconut milk.

INGREDIENTS

2-3	tbsp. olive oil
1	onion, finely chopped
2	garlic cloves, finely chopped
1	green bell pepper, sliced
1	red bell pepper, sliced
2	scallions, chopped
1	tsp. ground paprika
2	tomatoes, roughly chopped
1	14-ounce can chopped tomatoes
1	8-ounce can coconut milk
1	stem fresh thyme
¼	tsp. ground nutmeg
1	tsp. salt
¼	tsp. black pepper
1	pound white fish, cut in big pieces
3	tbsp. lemon juice
1	pound shrimp, peeled and deveined
1	bunch fresh cilantro finely chopped

DIRECTIONS

1. Heat the olive oil in a large pot. Add onion, garlic, peppers, scallions, and paprika, and sauté until onions are soft – about 7-8 minutes.

2. Next, add fresh tomatoes, canned tomatoes, and coconut milk, then the thyme, nutmeg, salt, and pepper, and bring to boil. Lower heat to simmer and add fish and lemon juice. Let simmer for 10 minutes.

3. Now add shrimp, tossing to coat, and simmer an additional 8-10 minutes, or until the shrimp are pink. Top with chopped cilantro and serve with white rice.

TIP

Coconut milk adds a distinct Caribbean flavor and sweetness to a hearty seafood soup.

TOTAL TIME:
1 HOUR
DIFFICULTY:
INTERMEDIATE
PORTIONS:
6 SERVINGS

VATAPÁ   [Vat-uh-PAH]

Spicy cream of seafood soup in peanut sauce

Vatapá shows the African influence in Brazilian cuisine, with shrimp cooked in a spicy, creamy peanut sauce. If you prefer, use evaporated milk instead of coconut milk.

INGREDIENTS

- 2 onions, finely chopped
- ½ cup dried shrimp (soak in warm water for 15 minutes, then drain)
- 2 garlic cloves, finely chopped
- 2 jalapeño peppers, chopped
- 1 tsp. turmeric
- ¼ tsp. shredded fresh ginger
- 3 tbsp. oil
- 1-2 cups water or fish stock
- ½ cup peanut or cashew butter
- 1 cup breadcrumbs, dried or homemade, unseasoned
- 1 pound shrimp, peeled and deveined
- 2 cups coconut milk or evaporated milk
- ¼ cup Red palm oil or sunflower oil

DIRECTIONS

1. Place the onions, dried shrimp, garlic, and jalapeño peppers, turmeric, and fresh ginger into a blender and puree well, adding a little water to blend well, making a puree consistency.

2. Heat the oil in a large saucepan over medium heat. Add the onion-shrimp mixture and sauté until cooked through, about 5-7 minutes.

3. Stir in the stock or water and whisk in the peanut or cashew butter until smooth. Then stir in the breadcrumbs, salt, and pepper. Bring to a boil, then reduce heat to low. Simmer for 5-8 minutes to meld the flavors.

4. Stir in the shrimp and coconut milk and simmer another 5-6 minutes, or until shrimp is pink.

5. Remove from heat, stir in the palm oil, and serve over white rice.

TIP

Vatapá is typical Bahian, with origins influenced by African, indigenous, and Iberean food styles, thus a wide assortment can go into the pot and still be considered 'authentic'. Usually bread is used to thicken it, though you could use manioc flour. Adding tomatoes, okra, or chiles would expand the other flavors.

TOTAL TIME:
1½ HOURS
DIFFICULTY:
INTERMEDIATE
PORTIONS:
6 SERVINGS

BOLINHO DE CHUVA   [Bow-LEE-no deh SHOO-vah]

Cinnamon doughnut holes

Bolinhos de chuva are small cinnamon doughnuts. The name directly translates to "little cakes of rain," and they are called this because they come out looking like little raindrops.

INGREDIENTS

½ cup, plus 3 tbsp. sugar

1 tbsp. cinnamon

1½ cups flour

½ cup cornstarch

¼ tsp. salt

2 eggs

½ cup buttermilk

½ cup milk

2 tsp. baking powder

Vegetable oil for frying

DIRECTIONS

1. In a bowl, stir in ½ cup sugar and cinnamon. Set aside.

2. In a big bowl, mix flour, cornstarch, 3 tablespoons sugar, and salt. Stir in eggs, buttermilk, and milk. Mix together with a wooden spoon, then fold in baking powder. Continue to stir until mixture has the consistency of a very thick batter.

3. Heat the vegetable oil over high heat. When the oil heats to 350° F, scoop generous teaspoons of batter and drop into the oil. Cook, turning occasionally, until golden brown.

4. Using a slotted spoon, remove cooked dough from the oil and drain over paper towels.

5. Roll the "raindrops" in the cinnamon sugar mixture while still hot. Serve immediately.

BRIGADEIRO   [BREE-gah-dehr-oh]

Chocolate truffles

These delicious chocolate truffles are a Brazilian favorite treat! Instead of chocolate sprinkles, consider rolling the treats in granulated chocolate, chopped pistachios or other chopped nuts, or powdered sugar.

INGREDIENTS

1 14-ounce can condensed milk

3 tbsp. unsweetened cocoa

1½ tbsp. butter

1 tsp. vanilla

Chocolate sprinkles to cover (good quality)

DIRECTIONS

1. In a saucepan, heat together the condensed milk, cocoa, and butter, stirring constantly until thickened, about 12 to 15 minutes. Remove from heat. Add vanilla and stir until completely blended.

2. Pour thickened mixture into a greased dish and set aside to cool. Fill a shallow dish with chocolate sprinkles.

3. Grease your hands with butter and roll the mixture into 1½-inch balls. Roll each ball in the chocolate sprinkles, to cover. Serve in paper baking cups.

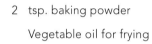

TOTAL TIME:
ABOUT 30 MINUTES
DIFFICULTY:
EASY
PORTIONS:
ABOUT 20 BALLS

TOTAL TIME:
30 MINUTES
DIFFICULTY:
EASY
PORTIONS:
20 SMALL BALLS

CHILE

Chile is a 2,600-mile-long ribbon of a country stretching along South America's western coast. It sits between the sapphire-blue Pacific Ocean and the white, snow-capped Andes Mountains.

Chile's northern region is predominantly arid desert. Yet each evening a dense sea mist known as camanchaca spreads up to fifty miles inland, providing vital moisture and causing a rapid drop in the hot midday temperatures.

There are more than 4,000 rocky islands and islets off the coast of southern Chile. Though dense evergreen rain forests provide some protection, these islands suffer the most furious of the sea's gales. Situated less than 600 miles from Antarctica, southern Chile is dotted with dozens of glaciers and ice fields. The intemperate conditions did little to deter the Germans who, starting in 1848, immigrated there in significant numbers. In addition to their culture, these Deutschlanders brought the pork dishes, sausages, and pastries that are now mainstays.

Chile's central valley is its great garden. Fruit orchards, olive groves, grape vines, and vegetables are harvested by the wagonful. During the dry season, roughly September through March, thousands of workers can be seen tending these crops. In addition to the native corn, potatoes, and beans, there are fields of tomatoes favored by Italian settlers, and plots of savory spices and herbs introduced by immigrating Arabs.

In 1888, Chile annexed Easter Island, making it the only South American nation to own a territory. Here the food offers a unique fusion of Polynesian and Chilean elements.

Even the British have played a part in Chile's culinary history. Chileans not only adopted té con leche (tea with milk) but also the social customs that accompany it.

Of course, the sea dictates much of Chile's food supply. The Humboldt Current runs the length of the Chilean coast bringing with it albacore tuna, salmon, swordfish, shellfish, squid, sea snails, and other delights.

Interestingly, perhaps more than in any other Latin American nation, hard-boiled eggs are a frequent ingredient in Chilean cooking. Cooks stuff them inside empanadas de pino along with beef, raisins, onions, and black olives. Coastal inhabitants enjoy boiled eggs with seaweed.

While Chile's diet has been inarguably shaped by immigration, the food of its indigenous peoples survives nationwide. Humitas, pureed corn cooked in husks, are Chile's unique take on tamales. Beans are used in dishes ranging from vegetable soups to seafood stews.

Like the nation itself, the following recipes are an exercise in contrasts. Follow this culinary trail to discover the full range of Chile's flavors.

EMPANADAS DE PINO   [Em-pah-NAH-thas Deh Pee-Noh]

Meat patties with vegetables

Chilean empanadas are adored throughout the country. Here, the "pino" refers to the filling: a seasoned mixture of ground beef, onions, raisins, black olives, and hard-boiled eggs.

INGREDIENTS

For the Pastry Dough:

3½	cups flour
1	tbsp. sugar
1	tsp. salt
1½	sticks cold butter, divided into small pieces
¼	cup ice water
1	egg

For the Filling:

2	tbsp. olive oil
1	onion finely chopped
2	garlic cloves, finely chopped
1	tsp. ground cumin
½	tsp. marjoram
¼	tsp. thyme
1	tsp. paprika
¼	tsp. preferred hot sauce (any hot sauce like Tabasco®)
1	pound ground beef
	Salt and pepper, to taste
¼	cup raisins
¼	cup black olives, chopped
2	hard-boiled eggs, chopped
1	egg white

DIRECTIONS

1. In a large bowl combine flour, sugar, and salt. Add butter in pieces and press into the dry ingredients with a fork. Add water and combine with hands until a dough is formed.

2. Turn the dough out on a clean work surface and flatten to a 1/8-inch thick rectangle. Then cut 12 4-inch discs from the rectangle. Wrap each disc in a plastic wrap and refrigerate for two hours.

3. While the dough is chilling, heat oil in a large skillet over medium-low heat. Add onions and cook until soft about 5 minutes. Add garlic, spices, and hot sauce. Add ground beef and cook until browned, about 8 to 10 minutes more. Add salt and pepper. Set aside to cool.

4. Preheat oven to 375° F. Remove dough from refrigerator. Line 2 baking sheets with parchment paper and set aside.

5. Lay out the dough rounds on a floured surface. Add 1 tablespoon of the meat mixture onto center of each dough round; then add raisins, olives, and eggs to each.

6. Using pastry brush or your fingertip, "paint" edges of dough with egg white. Fold one edge of the dough over toward the center, then fold another edge in, until a pocket is formed. Gently press down edges and press edges to seal.

7. Place empanadas on baking sheets, leaving 1½ to 2-inch spaces between them. Brush tops of empanadas with remaining egg wash.

8. Bake at 375° F until pastries puff and turn golden brown—about 20 minutes.

TIP

A complement to any meal and perfect as a grab-and-go snack.

TOTAL TIME:
2 HOURS
DIFFICULTY:
INTERMEDIATE
PORTIONS:
12 EMPANADAS

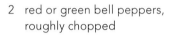

CURANTO [koo-RAHN-toh]

Shellfish, meat, and vegetables

Curanto has traditionally been prepared in a hole in the ground about 1½ yards deep, with the bottom of the hole covered with stones that were heated until ready. Nowadays it's generally prepared in a big pot on the stove – but there's no reason you can't invite some friends over and enjoy preparing this layered stew the customary way in a hole in your own backyard.

INGREDIENTS

3 tbsp. vegetable oil

4 garlic cloves, minced

2 onions, halved

2 red or green bell peppers, roughly chopped

1 tsp. ground cumin

1 tsp. tarragon

Salt and pepper

2 pounds chicken, with bones and skin, cut into 6-8 pieces

1 aji chili

1 whole cabbage

1 pound smoked pork ribs (if you can't find smoked ribs, you may use raw pork ribs)

4 pounds Yukon gold potatoes, whole unpeeled

1 pound chorizo or Italian sausage, cut into large pieces

2 pounds salmon, cut into large pieces

1 pound fresh mussels, cleaned well

3 pounds clams, cleaned well

1 bottle good white wine

4 bay leaves

DIRECTIONS

1. In a tall stockpot, heat oil over medium-high heat. Stir in garlic, onions and peppers and sauté until softened, about 5-7 minutes. Stir in cumin, tarragon, salt, and pepper.

2. Season chicken pieces with salt and pepper. Moving the vegetables to the sides of the pot, sear the chicken on both sides. Add bay leaves and whole aji chili to the same stockpot, mix, then cover with a layer of cabbage leaves.

3. For the second layer, add ribs, chorizo, and potatoes, seasoning with salt and pepper and covering with cabbage leaves.

4. Next, add the salmon and shellfish. Stir in white wine.

5. Reduce heat and let simmer for about 1 hour, or until the potatoes are done. Remove from heat and serve immediately in a big bowl.

TIP
Serve with rice and vegetable side dishes to capture the rich flavors.

TOTAL TIME:
2 HOURS
DIFFICULTY:
INTERMEDIATE
PORTIONS:
6-8 SERVINGS

PAILA MARINA   [PAHEE-lah mah-REE-nah]

Shellfish soup

This is a traditional seafood stew served in a paila, which is an earthenware bowl. The "marina" of course invokes the sea. This recipe calls for cod, but any firm white fish could be used in its place.

INGREDIENTS

- 3 tbsp. olive oil
- ½ onion, finely chopped
- 3 garlic cloves, finely chopped
- 2 medium tomatoes, chopped
- 1 tsp. salt
- ½ tsp. black pepper
- ½ tsp. oregano
- 1 tsp. paprika
- 1 pound cod, cut in bite-sized pieces
- ½ cup dry white wine
- 1 cup milk
- ¼ cup tomato sauce
- 1 pound mussels, cleaned, in shells
- ½ pound clams, cleaned, in shells
- ½ pound crab meat
- ¼ pound scallops
- 1 pound large shrimp, peeled and deveined
- 1 cup parsley, finely chopped

DIRECTIONS

1. Heat the oil in a large pot over medium-high heat. Stir in onions, garlic, and tomatoes, and sauté until soft, about 5-7 minutes. Stir, salt, pepper, oregano, paprika.

2. Add the cod, then the wine. Now gently stir in the milk and the tomato sauce. Cover and reduce heat to medium-low. Cook for 5 minutes.

3. Next, add mussels, clams, crab meat, scallops, and shrimps. Cook until the shells open and shrimp is pink.

4. Serve warm, in bowls, sprinkled with chopped parsley.

TIP

Filling and satisfying on its own, this soup gets its distinctive name from the serving bowl in which it is served. However, if no earthenware is available, you may still serve this soup and enjoy it heartily!

CHARQUICÁN   [Char-kee-KAHN]

Chilean beef stew

For a truly traditional experience, prepare this beef stew recipe with family and friends. To make a vegetarian version, eliminate the meat and use vegetable stock instead of beef stock. And to add another hint of authenticity, add a fried egg over each serving.

INGREDIENTS

2   tbsp. butter

1   pound stewing beef, cut into cubes

2   cups beef stock

3   ounces beef jerky, finely chopped

2   tbsp. olive oil

1   onion, finely chopped

3   garlic cloves, finely chopped

2   scallions, finely chopped

½   tsp. dry oregano

1   tsp. dry cumin

1   tsp. dry ground basil

½   tsp. chili flakes, chopped very finely

3   large potatoes, peeled and cut into cubes

1   butternut squash, peeled, seeded, and cut into cubes

1   cup carrot, peeled and cut into cubes

½   cup lima beans (canned, pre-cooked)

    Salt and pepper to taste

6   whole eggs, fried (optional)

DIRECTIONS

1. Melt butter in a large stockpot and add meat cubes. Sauté over medium-high heat until brown, about 5 minutes.

2. Pour in the stock and bring to a boil. Add the beef jerky and lower heat to simmer.

3. In a separate pan, warm olive oil. Then add onion, garlic, scallions and sauté until onion softens — about 5-7 minutes. Next, stir in spices and vegetables, and sauté an additional 5-7 minutes.

4. Add the sautéed vegetables to the stockpot. Cover and simmer over low heat for about 2 hours. Add lima beans to the pot and simmer 10 minutes more.

5. Season with salt and pepper and serve very hot, topping each serving with a fried egg, if desired.

TIP

Perfect on a rainy day, though meat and potato lovers would like this dish any day!

SOPAIPILLAS [soh-pahee-PEEH-yahs]

Fried pastry made with mashed pumpkin

It's a kind of quick bread. This is a typical fried snack that is easy to find from street vendors. During winter time people serve them with warm syrup. This snack bread can be picked up and eaten with your fingers.

INGREDIENTS

1½	cups sugar pumpkin (cooked and mashed)
4	cups flour
1	tsp. sea salt
1	tsp. brown sugar
2	tsp. baking powder
1	stick butter (melted)
1	cup oil for frying

Syrup

1	cup honey
½	cup water
2	cinnamon sticks
2	whole cloves
	Orange zest

DIRECTIONS

1. In a large bowl, mix together the flour, salt, baking powder, and brown sugar. Add the pumpkin mash and mix by hand gently until fully folded in. Add the melted butter little by little and mix the dough until it forms a ball.

2. Turn the dough out onto a lightly floured surface and knead until soft and homogenous (10-15 minutes). Cover and let it sit for 10 to 15 minutes.

3. Roll out the dough to about 1/3" thick, cut with 4" round cutter. Perforate rounds with a fork several times.

4. Heat the oil in a large, deep skillet. Fry the sopaipillas until golden brown on both sides, about 5 minutes, turning as they fry.

5. Turn out onto plate with paper towel to blot extra oil. Serve covered with warm syrup (or honey) or served on the side.

Syrup

In a small saucepan, combine all of the ingredients and cook over a medium heat until boiling. Reduce heat to low until mixture is a little thick. Drizzle warm syrup over sopaipillas.

TIP

Sopaipillas are best served with soups and stews as they are handy-helpers, capturing any gravy or sauce left on the plate.

TOTAL TIME:
1 HOUR
DIFFICULTY:
INTERMEDIATE
PORTIONS:
2 DOZEN

CALZONES ROTOS [Kahl-SOH-nehs ROH-tohs]

Dough twists with powdered sugar

These deep fried Chilean "underwear" cookies are especially good in wintertime when served with a creamy mug of hot chocolate.

INGREDIENTS

- 2 cups all-purpose flour
- ½ tsp. salt
- 1 tsp. baking powder
- ½ cup powdered sugar (plus extra for dusting)
- 2 eggs
- 1 egg yolk
- 1 tsp. vanilla extract
- 1 tsp. orange zest
- 3 tbsp. butter (room temperature)
- 2 tbsp. brandy
  Vegetable oil for frying

DIRECTIONS

1. In a bowl, whisk together dry ingredients. In another bowl, whisk together eggs, egg yolk, vanilla extract, and orange zest.

2. Fold dry ingredients into egg mixture. Add the softened butter and work the dough with your hands until well mixed. Next add the brandy, mixing with your hands.

3. Continue kneading the dough until all ingredients are mixed together. Cover the dough with plastic wrap and let rest for 20 minutes.

4. On a lightly floured surface, roll out the dough to about ¼ inch thick. Cut into 4 inch x 2 inch rectangles. Then holding each end of the dough rectangle, twist in opposite directions, gently pulling it up to shape the pastry.

5. Heat oil in a frying pan. When hot, fry cookies in batches for 3-4 minutes, until they are golden brown.

6. Remove cookies to a platter covered with paper towel. Dust with powdered sugar and serve immediately.

TIP

It is highly recommended to put a few on a plate and set a personal limit, or desire may get the better of one!

TOTAL TIME:
1 HOUR
DIFFICULTY:
INTERMEDIATE
PORTIONS:
15-18 COOKIES

MANJAR [Mahn-HAHR]

Caramel spread

This delicious caramelized milk spread is a variation of Dulce de Leche that can also be used as a pastry filling and even as a spread on bread, cheese, or cookies.

INGREDIENTS

4   cups half-and-half

1   cup sugar

1   vanilla bean, split lengthwise

1   tbsp. butter

¼   tsp. baking soda

DIRECTIONS

1. In a heavy saucepan, stir together the half-and-half, sugar, and vanilla bean over medium-high heat.

2. As soon as the half-and-half comes to a boil, reduce the heat to low and keep stirring until the milk turns a dark brown caramel color and thickens—about 1 to 1½ hours.

3. Gently stir in baking soda and continue to stir an additional 10 minutes.

4. Stir in butter and continue to stir an additional 5 minutes.

5. Scrape the manjar into a bowl and refrigerate until it's cool.

TIP

Manjar is similar to Dulce de Leche, though it utilizes half-and-half instead of milk. Spread on toast, it is a popular breakfast food enjoyed in Chile.

TOTAL TIME:
3 HOURS
DIFFICULTY:
INTERMEDIATE
PORTIONS:
1½ CUPS

COLOMBIA

Much like its geography, the cuisine of Colombia varies greatly. Connected to Panama by a small thread of land on its northwestern coast, the country is touched by both the Pacific Ocean and the Caribbean Sea.

The capital city of Bogota is located in a branch of the Andes range known as the Eastern Cordillera. At 8,600 feet above sea level it sits 3,000 feet higher than our "mile-high" city of Denver. Temperatures here average between 58 and 60 degrees, a fact that surprises many visitors.

In stark contrast, the lower third of the country is hot and humid. Here, the trees of the thick rainforest far outnumber people. The mighty Amazon River serves as Colombia's southern border.

Because Colombia offers both a temperate and a tropical climate, produce harvests are plentiful and varied. What we consider fall crops—tubers and root vegetables—grow year-round in the cooler mountain ranges. Closer to the seas, tropical crops flourish: bananas, coconut, dragon fruit, and lulos, which is an orange citrus fruit producing a much-loved green juice.

In the east, in the plains known as sabanas, cattle and hogs graze in abundance. These, as well as chicken and seafood, form the basis for the soups that are enjoyed all year in Colombia. Some are traditionally Spanish, incorporating rice and beans. Others are Caribbean influenced, relying on hot spices and both the meat and milk of the coconut.

Perhaps because sugarcane grows year-round in Colombia, sweet treats and beverages are well loved. Arequipe, which translates to "sweet milk jam," is a popular dessert spread. Hot chocolate, made from the nation's significant cocoa yield, is enjoyed throughout the day, as is coffee.

Unlike the flat tortillas associated with other Latin American countries, Colombia is known for unique corn cakes known as arepas. Thick, with a doughy center, they can be stuffed with meats and cheese, or fried to create a snack known as inflados.

The following sampling of Colombian cooking is a cross-country culinary tour. From the rice and coconut side dish to the minty avocado soup, you'll marvel at the broad range of flavors. Of course, there is no better way to end a meal than with arequipe, or Dulce de Leche, boiled and caramelized sweetened milk. Drizzle it over cakes or cookies, or just lick it off the spoon.

SOPA DE HABAS Y CEBADA   [SOH-pah deh HAH-bahs ee seh-BAH-dah]

Barley and fava bean soup

Originally from the Andean zone, barley and fava bean soup is a favorite comfort food in Colombia but also makes a nice dish for a Sunday brunch.

INGREDIENTS

- 1   onion, chopped
- 2   garlic cloves
- 2   scallions, chopped
- ½   green bell pepper, roughly chopped
- ¼   cup celery, roughly chopped
- 8   cups chicken or vegetable broth
- 1   cup fresh and peeled fava or lima beans
- ½   cup barley, soaked at least 1 hour and then dried
- 2   carrots, peeled and chopped
- 3   potatoes, peeled and chopped
- 1   cup chickpeas, fresh/raw
- ½   tsp. paprika
- ½   tsp. cumin

   Salt and pepper to taste
- ¼   cup fresh cilantro, chopped
- 1   ripe avocado, sliced

DIRECTIONS

1. Place onion, garlic, scallions, bell pepper, and celery in a blender and blend until smooth.

2. Pour broth into a large pot and add fava beans and barley. Bring to a boil then cook over medium high for 1 hour. Add water if needed.

3. Add blended mixture, carrots, potatoes, peas, paprika, and cumin. Reduce heat and simmer for 30 minutes, until vegetables and beans are tender.

4. Add salt and pepper to taste. Serve warm with fresh cilantro and avocado slices.

TIP

Wonderful with arepas (p. 62), which merges the chewy, rich corn flour biscuits with the liquid, legumes, grains and vegetables in this soup. Replacing chicken broth with vegetable makes this a vegan recipe.

TOTAL TIME:
2 HOURS
DIFFICULTY:
EASY
PORTIONS:
6-8 SERVINGS

ARROZ CON COCO [AH-rrohs Kohn KOH-koh]

Rice with coconut

This sweet and salty coconut rice recipe is a popular dish on the Caribbean coast of Colombia and usually served as an accompaniment to fried fish and patacones (fried green plantains).

INGREDIENTS

2	cups canned coconut milk
3	tbsp. brown sugar
1	tsp. salt
2-4	cups water
2	cups long grain rice
½	cup raisins

DIRECTIONS

1. In a heavy saucepan bring coconut milk to a boil over medium heat. Stirring constantly, reduce to low-medium heat, simmering for another 20 to 30 minutes, until liquid has evaporated and you can see the pulp. Continue cooking and stirring until liquid is completely evaporated and pulp browns.

2. Stir in brown sugar and salt. Now add 2 cups water, rice, and raisins. Bring the mixture to a boil until all liquid is absorbed and some small craters form on the surface (the rice will turn brown).

3. Cover the saucepan and reduce the heat to low for 20 minutes. Fluff the rice and serve hot.

TIP

Adding 1/4 cup of cranberries and 1/8 cup of shredded carrots will broaden the flavors while brightening up an otherwise traditional dish. Use for plating or as a garnish.

TOTAL TIME:
1½ HOURS
DIFFICULTY:
INTERMEDIATE
PORTIONS:
6 SERVINGS

AREPA CON POLLO ADOBADO [ah-REH-pah kohn POH-yoh ah-doh-BAH-doh]

Tortilla-style bread with marinated chicken

These corn griddle cakes with chicken are a versatile dish made often in Colombia. Here, the filling is made with shredded chicken as a base, but you can fill them with other shredded meats and spices such as beef with tarragon or pork with sage.

INGREDIENTS

- 2 cups corn flour
- ¼ tsp. salt
- 2 cups warm water
- ½ cup ricotta cheese
- 2 tbsp. olive oil
- 1 onion, finely chopped
- 2 garlic cloves, finely chopped
- 1 tsp. achiote
- 2 cups cooked and shredded chicken
- ½ tsp. cumin
- ½ tsp. oregano
- Salt and pepper to taste
- 1 ripe avocado, sliced
- 2 tbsp. fresh cilantro, chopped

DIRECTIONS

1. In a large bowl, mix together corn flour, salt, water, and ricotta cheese. Stir well, then knead with your hands to form a dough.

2. Divide the dough into 6 to 8 equal portions and form these into disks about ¼ inch thick and 4 to 6 inches wide.

3. Heat a griddle over medium heat. Place the disks on the griddle and cook about 5 to 7 minutes per side until they are golden and crisp. Remove from the griddle and set aside.

4. In a saucepan over medium heat, heat olive oil and add onion, garlic, and achiote. Sauté until soft—about 5-7 minutes. Next, stir in shredded chicken, cumin, oregano, and salt and pepper.

5. Fill the arepas with the warm chicken mixture and garnish with avocado slices and fresh cilantro.

TIP

Arepas are great as a side dish, a snack, or as the main event of the meal. Serve them with butter, cheese or hogao, a cooked mixture of onions and tomato. Arepas de huevo can be perfect for breakfast when the arepas are split open and stuffed with an egg.

TOTAL TIME:
1 HOUR
DIFFICULTY:
INTERMEDIATE
PORTIONS:
6-8 SERVINGS

ALMOJÁBANAS   [ahl-moh-HAH-bah-nahs]

Cheesy bread

A delicious "cheese bread" you can enjoy for breakfast or as a snack any time of day!

INGREDIENTS

1   cup ricotta cheese

1   cup cottage cheese

1   tbsp. butter, melted

1   cup masarepa corn flour
    (fine ground)

1   egg

3   tbsp. milk

½   tsp. baking powder

DIRECTIONS

1. Preheat oven at 400° F. Line a baking sheet with parchment paper and set aside.

2. In a large bowl, combine cheeses, butter, and masarepa flour. Add the egg, milk, and baking powder and mix well with a pastry blender or pastry cutter. Work with hands to form a dough.

3. Remove dough from bowl and divide into 6 to 8 equal parts; shape into balls. Place on parchment-lined baking sheet and bake for 25 to 30 minutes.

CREMA DE AGUACATE   [Kreh-mah deh ahgwa-KAH-teh]

Creamy avocado soup

This creamy avocado soup is perfect for lunch, a quick dinner, or an elegant dinner party appetizer served in a small bowl.

INGREDIENTS

3   ripe avocados, peeled and
    sliced

2   scallions, finely chopped

2   garlic cloves, finely chopped

1   tbsp. fresh mint

2   cups vegetable broth

2   cups heavy cream

    Salt and pepper, to taste

¼   cup fresh cilantro, finely
    chopped

¼   cup curly parsley for garnish

DIRECTIONS

1. In a blender, puree 2 of the avocados with the scallions, garlic, fresh mint and vegetable broth.

2. Pour pureed ingredients into a large pot over medium heat. Bring to a boil. Lower heat to medium and slowly stir in heavy cream and boil an additional 3 minutes.

3. Serve warm and garnish with remaining avocado slices, fresh cilantro, or parsley.

TOTAL TIME:
45 MINUTES
DIFFICULTY:
EASY
PORTIONS:
6-8 SERVINGS

TOTAL TIME:
30 MINUTES
DIFFICULTY:
EASY
PORTIONS:
6 SERVINGS

SANCOCHO TRIFÁSICO [sahn-KOH-choh tree-FAH-see-ko]

Three meat soup

A perfect weekend meal, this "three-meat" sancocho is a thick soup, almost like a stew, made with meats and root vegetables.

INGREDIENTS

6	chicken legs
1	pound pork ribs, cut into pieces
1	pound beef ribs, cut into pieces
1	tsp. salt
½	tsp. pepper
1	tsp. ground cumin
1	tsp. ground achiote
1	tsp. adobo
1	onion, peeled and quartered
1	red bell pepper, quartered
2	garlic cloves, finely chopped
3	ears fresh corn, each cut into 3 pieces
2	green plantains, peeled and chopped
4	medium potatoes, peeled and halved
1	pound fresh yucca peeled and cut into big pieces
1	pound pumpkin, chopped
2	tomatoes, seeded and chopped
¼	cup chopped fresh cilantro
2	ripe avocados, sliced

DIRECTIONS

1. Add meats, seasonings, onion, red bell pepper, and garlic to a large (16 or 20 quart) pot. Cover with water and bring to boil over medium heat. Cook, covered, for about 1 hour, or until meats are tender.

2. Reduce heat to low. Add corn, plantains, potatoes, yucca, and pumpkin, and simmer an additional 30 minutes, until vegetables are tender, and adding more water if necessary.

3. Remove from heat and stir in tomatoes. Divide the sancocho into bowls and garnish with fresh cilantro and avocado. Serve with white rice, if desired.

TIP

This soup gets its name from three different meats included in the pot at one time – chicken, pork and beef.

TOTAL TIME:
2 HOURS
DIFFICULTY:
INTERMEDIATE
PORTIONS:
6-8 SERVINGS

DULCE DE LECHE   [DOOL-seh Deh LEH-cheh]

Caramel

A treat also known as arequipe that is equally delicious over cookies, cake, or crackers – or even just by the spoonful!

INGREDIENTS

4	cups whole milk
1	cinnamon stick
1	clove
2	cups sugar
1	tsp. baking soda

DIRECTIONS

1. Pour milk into a medium pot and add the cinnamon stick, clove, and sugar. Bring to boil and reduce heat to low. Cook for about 1 hour, stirring constantly.

2. Add baking soda, keeping heat on low. Cook an additional 1 1/2 hours more, stirring often.

3. Remove from heat, strain, and pour into a glass bowl. When completely cool, cover and refrigerate for up to two weeks.

PLÁTANOS ASADOS CON BOCADILLO Y QUESO

[PLAH-tah-nohs ahs-SAH-dohs Kohn boh-kah-DEE-yoh ee KEH-soh]

Plantains with cheese

Baked ripe plantains with guava paste and melted cheese – a heavenly side dish, bursting with flavor!

INGREDIENTS

4	ripe plantains with skins
4	slices guava paste
4	slices mozzarella cheese
2	tbsp. crumbled parmesan
2	tbsp. melted butter
1	tsp. sugar
½	tsp. cinnamon

DIRECTIONS

1. Preheat oven at 400° F. Line a baking sheet with parchment paper and set aside.

2. Without peeling them, slice each plantain open lengthwise so that they resemble small "boats." Place the plantains on the baking sheet and bake for 30 to 35 minutes.

3. Remove from the oven and let cool. When cool, peel the skin off the plantains and add guava paste into the longwise cut. Cover with cheese, then brush with melted butter and sprinkle with sugar and cinnamon.

4. Place the stuffed plantains back in the oven and bake an additional 10 minutes. Sprinkle parmesan on top and serve immediately.

TOTAL TIME:
2½ TO 3 HOURS
DIFFICULTY:
INTERMEDIATE
PORTIONS:
8 SERVINGS

TOTAL TIME:
1 HOUR
DIFFICULTY:
EASY
PORTIONS:
4 SERVINGS

COSTA RICA

In Costa Rica, like most Latin American nations, life is celebrated with food.

Although smaller than the state of West Virginia, Costa Rica enjoys a diversity of climates unparalleled by other countries in the region. There are rainforests and volcanoes; beaches and mountain peaks high enough from which to view both coasts.

Corn, squash, cocoa and potatoes had been cultivated in Costa Rica for centuries before Christopher Columbus became the first European explorer to encounter them. It was Columbus who introduced sugarcane, rice, and other grains. He also brought the first cattle, hogs, and sheep to this country. The fertile soil and abundant fresh water proved well-suited to these newcomers, and they forever transformed Costa Rican food and its agricultural industry.

The warm and rainy northern Caribbean coast produces more bananas than nearly any other place in the world. African cultural influences can be seen—and tasted—throughout Limon and nearby provinces. Coconut and curry are added to create a unique rice and beans dish to serve with chicken or fish.

In Puntarenas, winding along the Pacific Ocean to the west, meals often come from the sea. Fresh caught tilapia and shrimp prepared with citrus juice are simple, delicious favorites.Maranon and caimito are two fruits that are very unique in that area. It is a must to stop for a "Chuchill" in Puntarenas.

San José, Costa Rica's capital, sits in the Central Valley in a province of the same name. It is the country's governmental, economic, and cultural hub. Traditional restaurants called "sodas" are abundant here with nearly all serving casados for lunch, the largest meal of the day. Casado translates to "marriage" and one look at the plate explains why. It is its own buffet with individual helpings of rice, beans, vegetables (such as potatoes, chayote, carrots with green beans), cheese and meat. Uncomplicated? Yes. Satisfying? Incomparably so.

The Costa Rican recipes to follow take you on both an historical and epicurean tour of this Central American jewel. Arroz con pollo, rice with chicken, illustrates the Spanish influence on the culture. Ceviche de Corvina, sea bass "cooked" in lime, evokes the flavors of the oceans that almost surround this nation.

Unlike some other Latin American fare, these dishes omit hot peppers and spices. But, as you'll soon learn, what Costa Rican food lacks in heat, it more than makes up for in variety.

GALLO PINTO [gah-YOH PEEN-toh]

Rice and beans

Popular throughout the country, Gallo Pinto (rice and beans) is a traditional dish generally enjoyed for breakfast and brunch. When served with fried or scrambled eggs, fried cheese, fried plantains, and tortillas, it's called "Casado" – which means "a complete meal."

INGREDIENTS

- 2 tbsp. vegetable oil
- 1 small onion, finely chopped
- 2 garlic cloves, finely chopped
- ½ bell red or green pepper, finely chopped

- 2 cups black or red cooked beans
- 2 tsp. Salsa Lizano or Worcestershire® sauce
- 1 tsp. salt
- 3 cups white rice, cooked
- 2 tbsp. cilantro, finely chopped

- Sour cream (optional)

DIRECTIONS

1. Heat oil in a pan over medium heat and sauté onion, garlic, and pepper for about 5 minutes. Add beans, Salsa Lizano, and salt.

2. Lower heat and simmer for about 5 to 8 minutes.

3. Add rice and cilantro and fold into other ingredients with a fork. Cover and continue to simmer an additional 10 minutes. Serve with sour cream on the side, if desired.

TIP

Costa Rican mornings are not complete without Gallo Pinto, which is simply considered "comfort food" by many.

CEVICHE DE CORVINA   [seh-BEE-cheh deh kor-VEE-nah]

Raw fish with lime

Raw sea bass "cooked" in lime juice is most popular in Puntarenas and Guanacaste, two provinces that are located on the Pacific side of Costa Rica.

INGREDIENTS

1½ pounds of raw white sea bass

1 cup fresh lime juice

½ cup orange juice

1 red onion, finely chopped

1 red bell pepper, finely chopped

3 tbsp. fresh cilantro, finely chopped

Salt and pepper, to taste

DIRECTIONS

1. Cut fish into ½-inch chunks and place in a glass dish.

2. Add the lime juice, orange juice, onion, pepper, and cilantro and toss to coat. Make sure the fish is completely covered by liquid. If not, add more lime juice.

3. Wrap with plastic and refrigerate for 6 hours or overnight. Toss and serve with crackers.

YUCA FRITA   [yoo-KAH FREE-tah]

Fried cassava

Fried yucca is an easy-to-make, delicious snack. The achiote or paprika is used for color. You can also opt to bake the yucca at 400° F for 30 minutes after you boil it. Just spritz it with a little vegetable oil first.

INGREDIENTS

2 pounds yucca or cassava, peeled and roughly chopped

½ cup vegetable oil

½ tsp. achiote or paprika

DIRECTIONS

1. Bring a large pot of salted water to a boil. Add peeled yucca and boil 25-30 minutes.

2. When yucca are soft, drain the pieces and run them under cold water to cool. Remove all the "string" and set aside.

3. In a deep fried pan, heat the oil and add the achiote or paprika. Now add the yucca pieces and fry on both sides until browned and crispy.

4. Remove to a paper towel-lined plate to drain excess oil and serve warm.

TOTAL TIME:
2½ HOURS
DIFFICULTY:
INTERMEDIATE
PORTIONS:
6 SERVINGS

TOTAL TIME:
50 MINUTES
DIFFICULTY:
EASY
PORTIONS:
4-6 SERVINGS

TAMALES [tah-MAHL-ays]

Steamed corn cakes in banana leaves

Tamales are a lot of work, a lot of flavor, and a lot of fun. One of the most unique Christmas traditions in Costa Rica is making tamales with family and friends.

INGREDIENTS

1	whole chicken
4	cloves garlic
½	onion
½	bell pepper
3	bay leaves
1	tsp. salt
½	tsp. black pepper
2	pounds pork ribs or pork loin
2	pounds instant corn masa mix (Maseca or Masarica)
2	pounds potatoes, cooked and mashed
½	250 ml. bottle Salsa Lizano or ½ cup of any Worcestershire® sauce
1	tbsp. salt
½	pound lard
4	pounds banana leaves
3	cups cooked rice seasoned with achiote or paprika
4	ounce package of raisins
40	green olives
40	pitted prunes
2	15-ounce cans sweet peas
2	15-ounce cans chickpeas
1	pound carrots, chopped into small pieces

DIRECTIONS

1. Place whole chicken in a large pot and add garlic, pepper, onion, salt, bay leaves, and black pepper. Cover with water and bring to a boil in medium high heat. Then cover and reduce heat to a simmer for about 1 ½ - 2 hours. When cooked, separate the meat from the broth. Shred the chicken into large pieces and set the broth aside.

2. Place pork in a different large pot and add garlic, pepper, onion, salt, bay leaves, and black pepper. Cover with water and bring to a boil over medium-high heat. Then cover and reduce heat to a simmer for 2-3 hours. When cooked, separate the meat from the broth. If you use the rib, leave the bone in the broth after cutting away the meat into medium-sized pieces; if you use the loin, remove all fat and shred the meat into approximately 2" pieces.

3. In a large saucepan, mix together the corn masa and mashed potatoes. Add chicken broth, pork broth, and Salsa Lizano. Mix well. Next, add 1 tbsp. salt and lard. Mix with hands to make a soft dough. If dough is not soft, add hot water.

4. Cut 40 of the banana leaves into squares. Spread flat 2-3 tbsp. of the masa dough in the center and fill (layer) with rice, about a tbsp. of shredded chicken, about a tbsp. of shredded pork, 2-3 raisins, 1 olive, 1 prune, 4-5 sweet peas, 4-6 chickpeas, and 2 pieces raw carrots. Fold the banana leaves and tie with a cotton string.

5. Cover the bottom of the pot with remaining banana leaves. Add the tamales and cover with water. Cook the tamales in gently boiling water for about 3 hours.

6. Unwrap tamales and serve warm with the banana leaves.

TIP

Saving the liquid, prepare the meat a day in advance, either in the morning or the day before.

TOTAL TIME:
7 HOURS
DIFFICULTY:
ADVANCED
PORTIONS:
40 TAMALES

GARBANZOS CON CERDO [gahr-BAHN-sohs Kohn sehr-DOO]

Chickpeas and pork

Chickpeas and pork stew makes a delicious one-pot "make-ahead" meal that can be reheated and enjoyed all through the week.

INGREDIENTS

- 6 cups water
- 2 cups dried chickpeas
- 2 pounds bone-in pork ribs, cut into pieces
- 3 tomatoes, quartered
- 3 garlic cloves, finely chopped
- 3 bay leaves
- 1 small onion, chopped
- ½ bell red pepper, chopped
- 1 stick celery
- 2 tsp. Salsa Lizano or any Worcestershire® sauce
- 1 tsp. salt
- 2 carrots, roughly chopped
- 3 tbsp. fresh cilantro, finely chopped

DIRECTIONS

1. Add all ingredients to a deep, large (16-20 quart) pot except for the salt, carrots, and cilantro. Bring to boil.

2. Once boiling, reduce heat to medium-low, cover, and cook for 3 hours, or until meat and chickpeas are well done.

3. Add carrots and salt and let them simmer in the stew for about 15 minutes. Remove from heat and sprinkle in cilantro. Serve warm.

TIP

Meat-on-the-bone enriches the soup base of these satisfying, nutritious legumes, making this the perfect dish for a mid-day meal. Chickpea and garbanzo beans are interchangeable terms and can be white or green, canned or fresh. If using fresh beans, soak them for 3 hours before using.

TOTAL TIME:
3½ HOURS
DIFFICULTY:
INTERMEDIATE
PORTIONS:
6-8 SERVINGS

ARROZ CON POLLO   [AH-rrohs Kohn POH-yoh]

Rice and chicken

A great recipe for rice and chicken – one of the main staples of Costa Rican food. Delicious with refried beans, this dish can be eaten for any occasion.

INGREDIENTS

1	small whole chicken
1	small onion, halved
3	whole garlic cloves
2	sticks celery
6	bay leaves
3	quarts + 1 1/2 cups water
2	tbsp. olive oil
1	tsp. achiote powder or paste
1	small onion, sliced
3	cloves garlic, finely chopped
1	red bell pepper, sliced
1	cup celery, finely chopped with leaves
2	cups long grain rice
1	tsp. salt
1	cup pitted green olives
½	cup raisins
1	can small peas
2	tbsp. Salsa Lizano (or Worcestershire® sauce)

DIRECTIONS

1. Add chicken, halved onion, whole garlic cloves, celery sticks, 3 of the bay leaves, and 3 quarts of water to a large pot. Set heat to medium. Bring to boil and continue boiling for about 1 ½ hours, or until chicken is soft enough to be shredded.

2. When chicken is done, remove from pot. Strain and reserve 1 cup of the broth for the rice. Shred the chicken and set aside.

3. Heat olive oil in a large saucepan over medium heat. Add achiote, sliced onion, chopped garlic, red bell pepper, and chopped celery and sauté until the onion and pepper are soft— about 5 to 7 minutes.

4. Reduce heat to medium-low. Add rice and salt and sauté about 3 to 5 minutes more. Then mix in the shredded chicken, olives, raisins, small peas, the remaining bay leaves, the cup of reserved chicken broth, and 1½ cups water and Salsa Lizano. Bring to a boil.

5. When liquid is reduced and the level of liquid reaches the rice, cover and reduce the heat to low for 30 minutes. Let rest 10 minutes more before serving.

TIP

The very last four ingredients in this dish create its distinctive flavor.

TOTAL TIME:
3½ HOURS
DIFFICULTY:
INTERMEDIATE
PORTIONS:
8-10 SERVINGS

SOPA NEGRA [SOH-pah NEH-grah]

Black bean and boiled egg soup

Black Bean Soup is a typical Costa Rican dish that will warm you from the inside – perfect for a cold day.

INGREDIENTS

2	cups raw black beans, soaked overnight
6	cups of fresh water
3	garlic cloves
1	stick celery
1	tsp. salt
2	tsp. vegetable oil
1	small onion
½	red or green pepper
6	hard-boiled eggs
2	tbsp. fresh cilantro
	Pepper to taste (optional)

DIRECTIONS

1. Add black beans to a large pot, along with 6 cups of fresh water, garlic, and celery. Bring to boil.

2. Once boiled, reduce heat to low, cover, and simmer for about 1 ½ to 2 hours or until beans are tender. If needed add an additional cup of water. When beans are soft, add salt and remove garlic cloves and celery stalk.

3. In a deep pan, heat vegetable oil. Sauté onion and pepper until softened. Add ½ cup cooked beans and mash them a little bit with a fork. Add the rest of the beans and liquid, then the hard-boiled eggs and bring to boil.

4. Reduce heat and simmer 5 to 10 minutes. Just before serving, sprinkle with cilantro and serve with white rice.

PUDÍN DE PAN [poo-DEEN deh Pahn]

Bread pudding

For an extra zip, soak the raisins 2-3 hours in a ¼ cup brandy before adding.

INGREDIENTS

4½	cups milk
3	cinnamon sticks
6	cups day-old white bread (or stale Brioche), cut into cubes
1	stick butter, melted
1½	cup sugar
¼	tsp. ground nutmeg
1	tsp. lemon zest
1	tbsp. vanilla
1	pinch of salt
5	eggs, slightly beaten
1	cup raisins
	Brandy, optional

DIRECTIONS

1. Preheat oven to 325° F.

2. In a large pot over medium heat, bring milk to a boil with the cinnamon sticks. When milk boils, remove cinnamon sticks and set milk aside.

3. In a large bowl, combine bread cubes with the boiled milk, the melted butter, sugar, nutmeg, lemon zest, vanilla, salt, and eggs. Mix well with a wooden spoon. Then add raisins and a splash of brandy, if desired.

4. Butter the bottom and sides of a glass baking dish and press the mixture into the dish. Place in oven and bake for about 45 minutes, or until a knife inserted 1 inch from edge comes out clean. Serve warm or cool.

TOTAL TIME:
4 HOURS
DIFFICULTY:
EASY
PORTIONS:
6 SERVINGS

TOTAL TIME:
1½ HOURS
DIFFICULTY:
EASY
PORTIONS:
8 SERVINGS

FLAN DE COCO   [FLAHN deh KOH-koh]

Coconut custard

The ingredients here combine beautifully to make a silky custard with a traditional Costa Rican flavor.

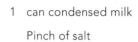

INGREDIENTS

2   cups sugar

5   eggs

1   cup evaporated milk

1   cup milk

1   can condensed milk

   Pinch of salt

1   tsp. vanilla

½   cup fresh coconut, shredded

DIRECTIONS

1. Bring 6 quarts of water to a boil in a large pot on the stove. While waiting for the water to boil, preheat oven to 325° F. When the water comes to a boil, pour it into a baking dish, filling it with enough boiling water to come half way up the sides of the dish. Transfer the dish to the oven.

2. Pour 1 cup of the sugar into a heavy-bottomed, medium-sized skillet, with the heat on medium-high until the sugar begins to melt. Stir continually while cooking; heat sugar until it melts and becomes a medium-dark brown, or about 5 minutes.

3. Remove from heat; pour caramelized sugar into a 9-inch round glass pie dish. Swirl dish until sugar evenly coats the bottom. Set aside and let cool.

4. Beat eggs in a blender. Then add the evaporated milk, regular milk, and condensed milk, remaining 1 cup of sugar, salt, vanilla, and shredded coconut, continuing to blend until combined.

5. Pour mixture into caramelized glass dish and set into dish with hot-water bath already in oven. Bake 45-50 minutes.

6. Remove from oven and let cool. Refrigerate at least 6 hours but it's better to let set overnight.

7. When ready to serve, place a serving dish on top of flan and invert. Slice and garnish with any remaining syrup.

TIP

This dessert can be served in individual portions, using small glass or porceline cups in step 5 instead of the large glass dish. The velvety smooth custard belies how little effort goes into the making.

TOTAL TIME:
4 HOURS
DIFFICULTY:
EASY
PORTIONS:
6 SERVINGS

CUBA

"In 1492, Columbus sailed the ocean blue..."

This old nursery rhyme supposedly taught children when Christopher Columbus discovered America. We now know, of course, that Columbus never reached what is today the United States — but he did, in 1492, first set foot in Cuba.

Cuba's history greatly influences its culture and cuisine. While Columbus introduced new foods and livestock to the Cubans, the Spaniards also introduced diseases to the indigenous Taino population. To replace this labor force, the Spanish brought African slaves to Cuba, descendants of whom remain today. In the early 1800s, the neighboring island of Haiti faced a revolution. Many Haitians escaped to Cuba, taking with them the cooking style of the French colonialists.

By the end of the 19th century, after Cuba won its independence from Spain, American tourists poured into the island nation. Many fell in love with the country's unique "mojo," a flavorful sauce made from olive oil, citrus juice, onions, garlic, and cumin. It is the finishing touch on nearly every dish—Cuba's answer to salt and pepper.

Cuba's semitropical climate enables abundant cultivation of fruits such as plantains and guava, and root vegetables like yams and yuccas. Surprisingly, though an island, seafood is less popular in Cuba than beef. Patiently slow-cooked, the result is a melt-like-butter, moist masterpiece.

As with most Latin American nations, rice and beans is a mainstay meal, although the preparation varies from area to area. Locally known as Arroz Congri—which translates to "Moors and Christians"—the dish perfectly represents the island's Spanish and African roots. Even today, the recipe depends on the cook. Some families simply boil the two ingredients together, while others bake their rice and beans with sautéed onions, sweet peppers, and garlic, and add some kind of pork meat.

Generally speaking, Cuban food is mild, not hot. Citrus is used as a marinade or cooking liquid, much as Americans use vinegar or meat broths. Salads are spare, but their limited ingredients allow each fresh vegetable's flavor to shine.

Unlike three-meals-per-day Americans, Cubans typically enjoy two hearty repasts: a breakfast served late morning and an evening dinner.

With the 1959 Cuban Revolution and subsequent embargo, dining habits on the island changed drastically. Frequent food shortages meant that cooks had to be flexible enough to use whatever resources might be available. The recipes in this chapter, however, reflect the full Cuban culinary palette, and Americans can easily find the ingredients needed.

ROPA VIEJA   [ROH-pah VEE-eh-hah]

Shredded steak

Ropa Vieja is considered a national dish of Cuba. This classic dish originated in Spain consisting of shredded flank meat in tomato sauce. A really easy yet dazzling main dish for dinner, slow cooking is the secret to its full flavor. Serve simply over white rice with black beans and some yucca on the side.

INGREDIENTS

3	tbsp. olive oil
1	onion, sliced
3	garlic cloves, finely chopped
½	red bell pepper, sliced into strips
½	green bell pepper, sliced into strips
2	pounds beef flank steak
1	16-ounce can tomato sauce
1	28-ounce can whole peeled tomatoes, crushed
½	cup red wine
2	cups beef broth
1	tsp. cumin
1	tsp. paprika
1	tsp. oregano
½	cup pitted green olives, chopped
	Salt and pepper to taste
	Fresh cilantro, chopped

DIRECTIONS

1. Heat oil in a large fry pan over medium high heat. Add onion, garlic, and peppers, and sauté for 5-7 minutes until soft.

2. Add the meat and brown 2-3 minutes per side.

3. Add tomato sauce, whole tomatoes, red wine, beef broth, spices, and olives. Bring to boil, then reduce heat to a medium-low. Cover and cook for about 3-4 hours or until meat is tender. Shred meat with a fork.

4. Add salt and pepper and pour shredded meat over white rice. Sprinkle with fresh cilantro and serve.

TIP

If you can't locate flank steak, try skirt steak, hanger steak, or London broil as options.

TOTAL TIME:
4 HOURS
DIFFICULTY:
EASY
PORTIONS:
6 SERVINGS

CROQUETAS DE JAMÓN [kro-KEH-tahs deh hah-MOHN]

Ham croquettes

Ham Croquettes are an authentic Cuban snack, generally served at parties like weddings and picnics. You can make the croquettes 3-4 days in advance; then cover with plastic, refrigerate, and save the frying for the day you plan to serve them.

INGREDIENTS

1½   cup milk

½   cup flour

¼   tsp. nutmeg

¼   tsp. black pepper

¼   tsp. salt

1   4-ounce stick butter

1   onion, finely chopped

2   cups ground ham (use a food processor or meat grinder)

3   eggs, lightly beaten

1   cup seasoned breadcrumbs

     Vegetable oil

DIRECTIONS

1. In a blender, mix together the milk, flour, nutmeg, pepper, and salt. Set aside.

2. Grind the ham in a food processor or meat grinder.

3. In a large skillet, sauté butter and onion for 2 minutes over medium-low heat. Reduce heat to low; add ground ham, mix well, and cook an additional 5 minutes.

4. Add milk mixture to skillet. Stir constantly until a dough is formed.

5. Remove the dough from the skillet and set aside until it comes to room temperature. Cover with plastic and refrigerate at least 4 hours.

6. When you are ready to make the croquettes, take 2 tsp. of dough into your hands and shape into logs. The mixture should make 12-15 croquettes.

7. One by one, dip each croquette into beaten eggs; then cover with the seasoned breadcrumbs. Repeat the process for each croquette.

8. In a fry pan, heat vegetable oil. When hot, add in the croquettes and deep fry for about 5 minutes until brown golden and crispy.

9. Place onto paper towel to drain the excess oil. Serve warm.

TIP

Salsa de Mojo Roja (p. 96) can serve as a complementary dipping sauce, with garlic and citrus flavors opening the ground ham and onion flavors within these sumptuous croquettes.

TOTAL TIME:
5½ HOURS
DIFFICULTY:
INTERMEDIATE
PORTIONS:
12-15 SERVINGS

FRIJOLES CUBANOS   [freeh-HOH-lehs kooh-BAH-nohs]

Cuban beans

Beans are the base of many meals in the Cuban culture. This dish originated in Spain but in Cuba shows an African influence.

INGREDIENTS

- 1 pound dried black or red beans
- 1 ham hock
- 3 bay leaves
- 3 tbsp. olive oil
- 1 onion, finely chopped
- 1 green bell pepper, finely chopped
- 4 cloves garlic, finely chopped
- 1 tsp. cumin
- 1 tsp. dried oregano
- 1 tsp. salt
- ½ tsp. pepper
- 1 tsp. sugar
- 1 tsp. red wine vinegar

DIRECTIONS

1. Wash the beans and place in a pot. Cover with water and store in the refrigerator overnight.

2. The next day, put the pot on the stove over medium heat. Add the ham hock and bay leaves. Bring to a boil, then reduce heat to medium-low. Continue boiling until beans are tender and water is reduced by half—about 2 hours.

3. In a medium saucepan, heat olive oil over medium heat. Add the onion, green bell pepper, and garlic and sauté until soft – about 5-7 minutes. Add cumin, oregano, salt, pepper, sugar, and red wine vinegar.

4. Add this sofrito to the beans and let boil for 10 minutes more, until all flavors are mixed. Serve warm.

TIP

Also known as frijoles negros, Cuban black beans are served at nearly every single meal in Cuba. Garnish the dish with chopped cilantro and chopped white onions, which make a great presentation and taste even better when mixed in.

The sofrito (onion, bell pepper, herbs and spices), is a traditional sauce used with so many dishes; prepare in advance and store in the refrigerator for up to 2 weeks.

TOTAL TIME:
2½ HOURS
(plus overnight
soak for beans)
DIFFICULTY:
EASY
PORTIONS:
6 SERVINGS

CHULETA DE PUERCO [choo-LEH-tah deh PWEHR-koh]

Grilled pork chops

A delicious, tangy take on pork chops.

INGREDIENTS

½ cup orange juice

¼ cup lemon juice

½ tsp. cumin

½ tsp. oregano

3 garlic cloves

½ tsp. salt

¼ cup red wine (optional)

6 thinly cut pork chops

1 tbsp. vegetable oil

2 onions, sliced

DIRECTIONS

1. In a medium bowl, combine orange juice, lemon juice, cumin, oregano, garlic, salt, and red wine (if using). Add pork chops in mixture to marinate. Cover the bowl and put it in the refrigerator overnight or at least 4 hours.

2. Heat the oil in a large skillet over medium-high heat. Add the pork chops one by one and fry about 5 minute per side, until brown. Remove pork chops from the skillet and set aside. Keep the drippings in the skillet.

3. In the same large skillet, sauté the onions for about 5 minutes. Pour the onions over the pork chops and serve immediately.

TIP

Orange and lemon juices are used to tenderize as much as flavor meats. Use a meat thermometer to determine done-ness with an internal temperature between 145° F (medium rare) and 160° F (medium), followed by a 3-minute rest.

TOTAL TIME:
30 MINUTES
(plus refrigerating
overnight)
DIFFICULTY:
EASY
PORTIONS:
8 SERVINGS

SALSA DE MOJO ROJA   [SAHL-sah Deh MOH-hoh ROH-hah]

Red Cuban sauce

Mojo Sauce is a versatile and delicious marinade for any meat, and an essential ingredient to making Cuban Sandwiches.

INGREDIENTS

6	garlic cloves	
½	tsp. salt	
½	tsp. pepper	
½	tsp. paprika	
1/3	cup fresh orange juice	
1/3	cup fresh lemon juice	
½	tsp. cumin powder	
¼	tsp. dried oregano	
1/3	cup olive oil	

DIRECTIONS

1. Using mortar and pestle, mash together the garlic, salt, and pepper, working it into a smooth paste.

2. In a small bowl, whisk together the orange juice, lemon juice, oregano, cumin, paprika, and the garlic paste made from previous step.

3. Heat the olive oil in a small saucepan over medium heat. When the oil warms, remove from heat and whisk the garlic-paste, spiced-juice mixture into the oil.

4. Cover and store in the refrigerator; bring to room temperature before using.

SANDWICH CUBANO   [SAHN-weehsh koo-BAH-noh]

Cuban sandwich

This classic Cuban sandwich is an easy meal as well as a crowd-pleaser. This recipe calls for ham and roasted pork, but you can use any pork or meat leftovers and still get a great result.

INGREDIENTS

2	tbsp. mayonnaise	
1/3	cup mojo sauce	
1	14-inch loaf Cuban bread or French baguette	
2	tbsp. mustard	
6	slices roasted sirloin pork	
6	slices fontina cheese	
6	slices ham	
6	slices tomato	
	Olive oil	
2	tbsp. butter, melted	

DIRECTIONS

1. Mix the mayonnaise with the mojo sauce.

2. Open the bread and layer with mustard, mojo and mayonnaise mixture, pork, cheese, ham, and tomato.

3. Heat a grill pan over medium heat and lightly coat with olive oil. Brush the sandwiches with melted butter on both sides.

4. Place sandwiches on the grill and press down firmly. Cook 4-6 minutes per side, until sandwich has compressed and bread is crispy.

5. Cut in 3-4 pieces. Serve warm with pickles.

TOTAL TIME:
25 MINUTES
DIFFICULTY:
EASY
PORTIONS:
4-6 SERVINGS

TOTAL TIME:
35 MINUTES
DIFFICULTY:
EASY
PORTIONS:
4 SERVINGS

FRITURAS DE YUCA [free-TOOH-rahs Deh yooh-KAH]

Yucca doughnuts

Yucca fritters are a favorite Cuban snack. Make these like mashed potatoes – but then bring it up a notch by frying and drizzling with honey. So yummy!

INGREDIENTS

1 pound yucca or cassava, peeled and cut into small pieces

¼ cup milk

1 stick butter

2 egg yolks, lightly beaten

¼ tsp. salt

2 tsp. sugar

¼ tsp. anise powder

Vegetable oil

Honey, for drizzling

DIRECTIONS

1. Put peeled yucca or cassava in a medium-sized pot and cover with water. Bring to a boil, and keep boiling over medium-high heat for 25 to 30 minutes or until yucca are soft.

2. Drain yucca, then mash into a puree, adding milk and butter as you do. Add egg yolks, salt, sugar, and anise powder. Set aside to cool.

3. When the yucca mash has cooled completely, form the mash into small 1 to 1-1/2-inch balls using spoon or melon-baller.

4. Heat vegetable oil in a large pan to 325° F. Fry the balls about 10 minutes, until browned. Remove with a slotted spoon onto a paper-towel lined surface. Drizzle with honey and serve.

TIP

These delightful doughnuts "puff up" while frying and expand to double their original size.

TOTAL TIME:
1½ HOURS
DIFFICULTY:
INTERMEDIATE
PORTIONS:
12-15 BALLS

MEXICO

Only a few generations ago, American visitors to Mexico were still perplexed by our southern neighbor's cuisine. The flavors were unusually bold; the presentation unfamiliar. One early travel writer, when confronted with a bowl of chili con carne, thought it was soup. He didn't understand why it was so thick, or why it contained diced red peppers. Imagine his amusement had he been told the "soup" he found so odd would one day become an international comfort food.

Even today there are many who assume that Mexican food consists of little more than corn tortillas, black and brown beans, and spicy sauces. While these are certainly national staples, this short-sighted culinary view belies a tasty truth: Mexican food is one of the world's first "fusion cuisines." Drawing from its multi-cultural past, Mexican meals are as diverse as they are delicious.

Mayans, one of the earliest inhabitants of the region, began cultivating maize (corn) nearly 5,000 years ago. Aztecs harvested beans, avocados, sweet potatoes, and other vegetables. Their unique blending of chocolate, chili peppers, and salt are still replicated by 21st century cooks.

The Spanish invaded Mexico in the early 1500s. They introduced horses, cattle, sheep, hogs, rice, citrus fruit, spices, and wheat flour to the Mexicans—but, in actuality, many of these were second-hand contributions. The Moors—who ruled Spain for 700 years—used rice and saffron in nearly every meal. The conquistadors merely adopted these ingredients and passed them on. Likewise, returning Spaniards presented Mexico's cocoa beans and coffee to the Europeans.

With each preceding culture, Mexico's flavor-bending recipes became more nuanced and distinctive. Vegetables indigenous to the New World, like squash and tomatoes, were added to Spanish dishes. Mexican meals were modified with the introduction of new meats like pork and beef. Spanish cooking techniques, including frying, further expanded Mexican cuisine.

Today, Mexican food is a hybrid of flavors and methods found nowhere else in the world. Christmas is celebrated with tamales stuffed with meats, cheeses, or even sweet fruits like pineapple. Mexican hot chocolate is a creamy delight thickened with corn flour and sweetened with natural cane sugar. Shrimp is ceviched in lemon juice. Fish is fried and folded into tacos. Diners expecting only beans and rice are in for a pleasant surprise indeed.

The following dishes feature an appetizing cross-section of Mexican fare. They range from quintessential snacks like cheese enchiladas, to zesty Mexican-style breakfast eggs known as huevos rancheros to the complex and delicious mole sauce that makes any meal a delicacy. Though some of these recipes are thousands of years old, you'll find the flavors still incredibly fresh and satisfying.

HUEVOS RANCHEROS [HUEH-vohs rahn-CHEE-rohs]

Mexican-style eggs

Mexican-style eggs is a very popular dish for breakfast, but especially good for a weekend brunch. Serve eggs over-easy or sunny-side-up, depending on your preference.

INGREDIENTS

Vegetable oil

1   onion, finely chopped

3   garlic cloves, finely chopped

1   jalapeno pepper,
    finely chopped

4   tomatoes, chopped

1   14 1/2-ounce can of
    tomato sauce

1   tsp. hot sauce

    Salt and pepper, to taste

6   eggs

6   corn tortillas

½   cup white (queso fresco)
    cheese, crumbled

¼   cup fresh cilantro,
    finely chopped

DIRECTIONS

1. In a large skillet, heat oil then sauté onion, garlic and jalapeno pepper, until soft, about 5 to 7 minutes.

2. While onion, garlic, and jalapeno pepper are cooking, add oil to a separate skillet and heat. Add tortillas, one by one, to skillet, toasting about 3 seconds per side. Remove and set aside.

3. Stir in fresh tomato and tomato sauce and bring to boil. Reduce heat to medium-low and season with hot sauce, salt, and pepper. If needed, add 2-3 tbsp. water.

4. Break eggs, one by one, over tomato sauce. Cover and simmer over low heat until eggs are done, about 5 minutes for sunny-side-up.

5. Serve over fried tortillas and garnish with cheese crumbs and fresh cilantro.

TIP

Gently pan-fry corn or wheat tortillas in a separate skillet to crisp-up before serving.

TOTAL TIME:
35 MINUTES
DIFFICULTY:
EASY
PORTIONS:
6 SERVINGS

ENCHILADA DE QUESO [ehn-chee-LAH-thah deh KEH-soh]

Corn tortillas with sauce and cheese

A cheese enchilada is a quintessential Mexican treat, but you can also stuff it with shredded chicken or meat.

INGREDIENTS

2	dry chili ancho peppers
6	tomatoes
2	garlic cloves
1	tsp. dried oregano
1	tsp. dried cumin
½	cup water
¼	cup vegetable oil
12	corn tortillas
1	cup shredded white cheddar cheese
1	cup shredded yellow cheddar cheese

DIRECTIONS

1. Preheat oven to 350° F.

2. Place the dry chili ancho peppers in a medium bowl. Cover with water and set aside for a half hour to hydrate. Drain.

3. In a large saucepan combine the hydrated ancho chili peppers with tomatoes. Cover with water and bring to boil. Reduce heat to a simmer and cook for about 15 minutes. Remove the tomatoes and set aside. Cook peppers 10 minutes more. Drain.

4. Place tomatoes and peppers in a blender, adding the garlic, oregano, and cumin. Puree until blended.

5. Pour this mixture into a saucepan and add ½ cup water. Bring to a boil, and keep boiling for about 10 minutes. Set aside to cool.

6. While the sauce is cooling, heat oil in a large fry pan over medium heat. When oil is hot, add one tortilla at a time and cook 2-3 seconds per side. Repeat process with all the tortillas. Place cooked tortillas on a plate covered with paper towel. Set aside.

7. Spread tomato sauce on one side of the tortillas. Combine 2 different cheeses and add to the middle, roll up the tortilla, and place in casserole dish. Repeat until all tortillas are filled.

8. Add the rest of the sauce over the rolled tortillas. Sprinkle the rest of the cheese over the top.

9. Bake at 350° F for 20 minutes or until cheese is melted and golden. Serve warm.

TIP

In Mexico, the custom is to make enchilada sauce in "molcajete," an authentic Mexican mortar also used to grind and crush spices and prepare salsas and guacamole.

TOTAL TIME:
1 HOUR
(after chili peppers
are hydrated)
DIFFICULTY:
INTERMEDIATE
PORTIONS:
6-8 SERVINGS

FAJITAS DE POLLO [fah-HEE-tahs deh POH-yoh]

Chicken marinated with onions and peppers

A Mexican dish made with strips of chicken or beef. The base of this dish is marinated meat which is then cooked like stir-fry. Chicken fajitas are usually served on a cast-iron pan with warm tortillas and pico de gallo sauce on the side.

INGREDIENTS

- 4 tbsp. vegetable oil
- 2 tbsp. lemon juice
- 3 cloves garlic, finely chopped
- ½ tsp. oregano
- ½ tsp. crushed red pepper flakes
- Pinch of salt
- 3 boneless, skinless chicken breasts, cut into chunks
- 2 onions, thinly sliced
- 1 red bell pepper, thinly sliced
- 1 yellow bell pepper, thinly sliced
- 1 green bell pepper, thinly sliced
- Salt and pepper, to taste
- 4 tortillas
- Fresh cilantro, finely chopped

DIRECTIONS

1. In a bowl, add 2 tbsp. vegetable oil, lemon juice, garlic, oregano, red pepper flakes, and ¼ tsp. salt.

2. Toss pieces of chicken in marinade, cover, and refrigerate for 2-4 hours.

3. In a large skillet, over medium heat, sauté onion and peppers until tender, about 5-7 minutes. Remove from skillet and set aside.

4. Add chicken to the same skillet. Cook the chicken on medium-high heat for about 8 minutes, or until tender. Add onion and pepper mixture back to the pan. Serve immediately, with warm tortillas on the side and garnish with fresh cilantro.

TIP

Methods for heating tortillas

Cast iron or skillet method: Place the tortillas one by one in a dry, medium-high pan. They will puff up, soften, and toast; flip to both sides.

Oven Method: Wrap 6-8 tortillas in tin foil and place in pre-heated 350° F oven for 15-20 minutes.

BBQ Method: Place the tortilla on the grate above cooled coals for literally just a few seconds on each side. Flip by using tongs. Adds exceptional flavor.

TOTAL TIME:
30 MINUTES
(plus marinating time)
DIFFICULTY:
EASY
PORTIONS:
4 SERVINGS

FLAUTAS DE POLLO CON SALSA DE AGUACATE

[FLAÚ-tahs deh POH-yoh Kohn Sal-ZA deh AGWA-kah-teh]

Rolled tortilla stuffed with shredded chicken

The term "flauta" is derived from the Spanish word for flute. Flautas can be made with any meat, but they have to be crisply fried to be authentic.

INGREDIENTS

Vegetable oil

2 skinless, boneless chicken breast and thighs

2 garlic cloves

1 bay leaf

1 tsp. paprika

½ tsp. salt

¼ tsp. pepper

12 corn tortillas

1 ripe avocado

½ cucumber

1 tsp. lemon juice

Fresh cilantro for garnish

Sour cream (optional)

DIRECTIONS

1. Heat 1 tbsp. of oil in a medium pot over medium-high heat. Add chicken. Cover half-way up with water.

2. Add garlic, bay leaf, paprika, salt, and pepper. Bring to a boil, reduce the heat to low, and simmer until chicken is tender, about 20 minutes.

3. Remove the chicken from the pot and shred with a fork. Add one tbsp. of shredded chicken into each tortilla. Roll the tortilla tightly around the filling and secure with toothpick.

4. In a blender, add avocado, cucumber, and lemon juice. Puree well and add salt and pepper to taste. Set aside.

5. Add ½ cup more oil to a medium skillet and heat. When oil is hot, fry the flautas, no more than 2-3 at a time, for 2-3 minutes for each side or until crispy and golden.

6. Remove flautas from skillet and place on a plate lined with paper towel.

7. Place flautas in a server plate. Remove the toothpicks. Cover with avocado sauce and cilantro. Serve with sour cream on the side, if desired.

TIP

Garnish with crumbled queso blanco or white cheese. Grated cheddar tastes equally good, though it is a sharper flavor.

TOTAL TIME:
45 MINUTES
DIFFICULTY:
EASY
PORTIONS:
4-6 SERVINGS

NACHOS   [NAH-chohs]

Tortilla chips with toppings

Nachos are originally from the city of Piedras Negras in Northern Mexico, just south of the border from Eagle Pass, Texas. This is a special snack that is very easy to make and very easy to eat!!! Special to share with friends and family at any occasion or reunion.

INGREDIENTS

1	tbsp. olive oil or vegetable oil
1	onion, finely chopped
3	cloves garlic, finely chopped
½	chili pepper, finely chopped
1	tomato, finely chopped
1	pound sirloin, thinly sliced or ground
1	tsp. cumin
½	tsp. thyme
½	tsp. paprika
	Salt and pepper, to taste
	Tortilla chips
1	cup shredded cheddar cheese
	Sour cream, optional
	Guacamole, optional (see p. 112)

DIRECTIONS

1. Heat oil in a large skillet over medium heat and sauté onion, garlic, and chili pepper.

2. When ingredients are soft, after about 5-7 minutes, add tomato. Next, stir in meat and mix all the ingredients together with a wooden spoon.

3. Reduce heat. Season with cumin, thyme, paprika, and salt and pepper. Simmer for 8-10 minutes more. Set aside.

4. Arrange tortilla chips to cover a large plate. Cover the chips with half the cheese. Add meat, then add the rest of the cheese. Serve with sour cream and/or guacamole.

TIP

Nachos are sometimes served with ground chicken or shrimp instead of beef. Raw jalapeño peppers can be added as a garnish if "extra spicy" is called for.

TOTAL TIME:
45 MINUTES
DIFFICULTY:
EASY
PORTIONS:
6 SERVINGS

GUACAMOLE [gwa-kah-MOH-leh]

Avocado dip

This traditional and versatile snack is good eaten with tortilla chips but also makes a nice sauce over tacos, fajitas, or any Mexican food.

INGREDIENTS

4 ripe avocados

Juice of 1 lime

1 onion, finely chopped

½ tsp. Tabasco®
(or any red sauce)

Salt to taste

½ jalapeño pepper, very finely chopped (optional)

Fresh cilantro, for garnish

DIRECTIONS

1. Cut avocados in half and remove the pits. Reserve one pit for later. Use a spoon to scoop out "meat" and place in a bowl. Mash avocados with a fork or use a molcajete to crush.

2. Add lime juice, onion, red sauce, salt, and jalapeño pepper, if desired, and toss ingredients together well. To prevent browning, add one pit and remove just before serving.

3. Garnish with fresh cilantro and serve with tortilla chips.

TIP

For even more flavor, add one chopped tomato during step 2.

TOTAL TIME:
15 MINUTES
DIFFICULTY:
EASY
PORTIONS:
4-6 SERVINGS

MOLE   [MOH-leh]

Traditional Mexican sauce

This traditional and versatile snack is good eaten with tortilla chips but also makes a nice sauce over tacos, fajitas, or any Mexican food.

INGREDIENTS

- 4   cups chicken broth
- ¼   cup vegetable oil
- 2   ancho peppers, stemmed and seeded
- 2   pasilla peppers, stemmed and seeded
- 2   chipotle peppers, stemmed and seeded
- 1   onion, finely chopped
- 2   whole garlic cloves
- 2   tomatoes
- 2   tomatillos (green tomatoes)
- 2   tsp. sesame seeds
- 1   tsp. coriander seeds
- ¼   cup pumpkin seeds
- ¼   cup white almonds
- ¼   cup peanuts
- ¼   cup raisins
- 2   cinnamon sticks
- 3   cloves
- ½   orange peel
- 4   ounces bitter dark chocolate
- ¼   tsp. thyme
- ¼   tsp. sugar
- ½   tsp. salt

DIRECTIONS

1. Pour chicken broth into a large pot and bring to a boil. Once it boils, lower the heat and simmer 5 minutes. Remove from heat and set aside.

2. In a medium-sized pan, heat oil over medium heat. When the oil is hot, add the peppers to toast for about 3 minutes. They are done when they are warm and aromatic. Transfer to a blender and puree into a paste.

3. In the same pan with the same oil, sauté onion and garlic, until soft—about 5-7 minutes. Now stir in tomatoes, tomatillos, and all the seeds plus the almonds, peanuts, and raisins, and cook for 2-3 minutes more.

4. Stir in cinnamon sticks, cloves, and orange peel. Now add the pepper paste, the chocolate, thyme, sugar, salt, and the reserved chicken broth. Simmer for about 12-15 minutes. Turn off the heat. Cover and let the mix rest for 30-40 minutes.

5. Remove cinnamon sticks, cloves, and orange peel and puree the remaining ingredients in blender.

6. Pour out of blender and serve immediately over meat, tacos, flautas, or what have you. Can be refrigerated for up to a month. When you are going to use it, add a little chicken broth to soften.

TIP

Try mole on the Thanksgiving turkey, it is amazing. Set the bird on a rack in a suitably-sized pan, spread softened butter under the skin and use a brush or your fingers and spread mole sauce over the entire outside of the bird. Roast as you would otherwise, and thoroughly enjoy!

TOTAL TIME:
2 HOURS
DIFFICULTY:
ADVANCED
PORTIONS:
8 SERVINGS

CREPA DE CAJETA [KREE-pah deh kah-HEH-tah]

Crepe with caramel

Cajeta crepes originated in Guanajuato, but are very popular all over the country. Consider upping the appeal by adding nuts, fresh banana slices, or even ice cream over each crepe.

INGREDIENTS

1   cup milk

1   tsp. vanilla extract

2   eggs

1   cup flour

2   tbsp. butter, melted

½   cup heavy cream

1   tbsp. rum

1   cup Dulce de Leche

DIRECTIONS

1. In a bowl, whisk together milk, vanilla extract, and eggs. Stir in flour, mixing well, then pour in melted butter.

2. Heat a lightly greased pancake skillet. Add 1 ½ tbsp. batter and spread batter evenly over the skillet. Cook until the batter bubbles—about 2 minutes per side. Repeat until all batter is used. You should end up with 6 crepes.

3. Keep the crepes in a container, adding a paper towel or sheet of waxed paper between the crepes.

4. Now heat heavy cream in a medium pot. When the cream starts boiling, add ½ cup of the Dulce de Leche, stirring constantly until boiling again. Stir in rum and set aside.

5. Fill each crepe with a tsp. of the Dulce de Leche sauce and fold in half, then fold in half again. Spread all over with sauce. Top with fresh fruit or a scoop of ice cream, if desired, and serve warm.

TIP

Light, flavorful and able to manage a variety of toppings, serve these for brunch or midnight snack.

TOTAL TIME:
45 MINUTES
DIFFICULTY:
INTERMEDIATE
PORTIONS:
6 CREPES

PERU

Solanun tuberosem.

You may not be familiar with this Peruvian species of potato, but it is the ancestor of nearly all potatoes cultivated worldwide. It is but one example of the breadth of Peru's culinary influence on societies around the globe.

Once the home of the Incas, Peru's native civilization was socially, politically, and agriculturally advanced. In addition to potatoes, they nurtured both lima beans and sweet potatoes, food stuffs unique to their region. When Spaniards introduced Mexico's corn and chili peppers, early Peruvians developed their own varieties.

Like other Latin American nations, European immigration was particularly strong before and after the world wars. Another interesting influence is a Chinese-based cuisine called "chifa", a culinary tradition based on creating Chinese-Cantonese flavors with traditional Peruvian ingredients and traditions. Because traditional Asian ingredients are scarce, they have been replaced with Peruvian staples. The result is a wonderfully unique fusion of two powerful taste profiles.

Although only about one-seventh the size of South America's largest country, Brazil, Peru is divided into three very distinct climate zones. The people of the Pacific Coast, which forms the nation's western border, subsist mainly on seafood. Cooked any number of ways, recipes often call for spicy peppers and the fresh, tart juices of citrus fruit. In the Andes mountains, herds of alpaca are grown for both wool and meat. Sheep, cattle, and pigs graze in the fertile valleys between the slopes while corn, potatoes and other vegetables grow abundantly in the rich, loose soil. Lastly, there is the Amazon region. The Amazon River teams with food sources, including the arapaima, one of the largest freshwater fish in the world. A typical specimen can yield nearly 150 pounds of edible meat. Even piranha are caught and fried.

Ceviche is a flagship dish of Peru, with sea bass the favored protein. The fish is not cooked with heat but rather by refrigerating the filets in lime juice and other seasonings for several hours. Typ-

ical side dishes include sweet potatoes or round slices of grilled corn on the cob.

Sweet dishes and desserts are popular in Peru. Arroz con leche—rice with milk—is a favorite. The lúcuma fruit, almost exclusive to the Andes region, is probably the most universally enjoyed dessert. It is made into ice cream and milk shakes, or simply cooked down to a syrup somewhat reminiscent of maple syrup.

Whether you start with Peru's cold, mashed potato picnic dish causa limena, or the Chinese- influenced beef dish lomo salteado, the following recipes prove why Peru is a world leader in creative culinary fare.

PAPAS A LA HUANCAÍNA [PAH-pahs ah lah wahn-ka-EE-nah]

Peruvian potatoes with spicy sauce

This is a popular dish in the summer. If you want to reduce the heat, boil the aji chili peppers 3 to 5 minutes before starting.

INGREDIENTS

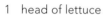

- 3 tbsp. olive oil
- 1 red onion, chopped
- 2 garlic cloves, chopped
- 3 yellow chili peppers, cleaned
- 1 cup evaporated milk
- 3½ ounces farmer's cheese
- 6 Ritz crackers
- Salt and pepper to taste
- 1 head of lettuce
- 6 large white or yellow potatoes, peeled, boiled and sliced
- 3 hard-boiled eggs, sliced, for garnish
- Black olives, for garnish

DIRECTIONS

1. Heat olive oil in a skillet. Sauté onion, garlic, and yellow chili peppers in olive oil for about 5-7 minutes, or until soft. Set aside to cool.

2. In a blender, mix together evaporated milk and cheese. Add cooled yellow chili mixture, crackers, and salt and pepper, and continue to blend together.

3. Wash the lettuce well and separate the leaves. Place the leaves on a platter. On top of that, add potato slices. Pour sauce over potatoes and garnish with hard-boiled eggs and black olives.

TIP

In Peru, the potatoes take center stage while hard-boiled eggs complement this dish.

TOTAL TIME:
30 MINUTES
DIFFICULTY:
EASY
PORTIONS:
4 SERVINGS

CEVICHE PERUANO [seh-BEE-chay peh-ROOAH-noh]

Raw fish bits cooked in lemon and spices

Ceviche is an old tradition in South America, dating back from the Incas. Raw fish is tossed with freshly squeezed lime juice and spices, which changes the texture of the fish, or "cooks" it, without changing its flavor.

INGREDIENTS

1   pound fresh sea bass, cut into ½ inch chunks

3/4   cup freshly squeezed lime juice

1   tsp. salt

½   tsp. pepper

½   yellow aji chili pepper, seeded and cut into 2 pieces (optional)

1   red onion, cut into thin strips

2   tbsp. fresh cilantro, chopped

2   sweet potatoes, boiled, peeled and sliced into ¼-inch-thick rounds

DIRECTIONS

1. Rinse the fish with cool water. Pat dry.

2. Place the raw fish pieces in a clean glass bowl. Add the lime juice, salt and pepper, and aji pepper, if desired. The fish should be completely covered by the lime juice.

3. Place in the refrigerator and marinate for at least 4 hours, stirring occasionally.

4. Remove from refrigerator and add onion and cilantro. Toss well. Remove the aji pepper, if used.

5. Serve ceviche in individual bowls over slices of sweet potato.

TIP

If sea bass (either white or black) is not available, a standard ceviche fish is Pacific rockfish or lingcod that's been pre-frozen. Any sort of snapper, grouper, porgy, sea trout, or yellowtail will work.

TOTAL TIME:
4½ HOURS
DIFFICULTY:
EASY
PORTIONS:
4 SERVINGS

CHUPE DE CAMARONES [CHOOH-pe deh kah-mah-RHO-nehs]

Shrimp soup

Chupe is the Peruvian national dish, a delicious seafood soup. It is served for many occasions and can be a side dish or the main meal.

INGREDIENTS

2 pounds large shrimp, with shells and heads (reserve the shells and heads to make a broth)

3 large potatoes, diced

1 large carrot, peeled and diced

1 cup squash, diced

1 cup habas (broad beans)

1 large tomato, diced

2 tsp. tomato paste

2 ears of corn, husked, in chunks (1")

½ cup rice

4 eggs

½ cup fresh cheese (white cheese)

1 cup heavy cream or half and half

1 red onion diced

4 cloves garlic, finely chopped

1 tsp. cumin

2 tsp. fresh oregano, chopped very finely

1½ tsp. aji panca

1 tsp. aji amarillo

4 cups shrimp broth (made with shrimp's heads and shells)

2 tsp. oil

Salt and pepper to taste

DIRECTIONS

1. Clean the shrimp, removing the shells and heads and refrigerate the shrimp. Reserve the shells and heads to make the broth.

2. Put the heads and shells in a medium saucepan, cover with 5-6 cups of water and let boil, then cover and simmer for 20 minutes, strain and set aside. Be sure the liquid measures to at least 4 cups of broth.

3. Heat olive oil over medium high heat, add garlic and onion and cook until tender. Add tomato paste, aji amarillo and aji panca, toss well and reduce heat.

4. Add tomatoes and cook for about 3 to 5 minutes, then add shrimp broth and bring it to a boil.

5. Add rice, habas, corn chunks, carrots, and squash. Reduce heat to a simmer and let simmer for about 10 minutes.

6. Add potatoes, add salt to taste and simmer 10 to 15 minutes more.

7. When potatoes and rice are just tender, add in the shrimp and cook until they turn pink, about 3 to 4 minutes. Add the cream and cheese and continue stirring. When the soup begins to boil, crack the eggs into the soup and cook about 3 to 4 minutes more and it's ready. Sprinkle with fresh oregano and serve.

TIP

If you want you can use evaporated milk instead of cream or half and half.

TOTAL TIME:
1½ HOURS
DIFFICULTY:
INTERMEDIATE
PORTIONS:
6 SERVINGS

CAUSA LIMENA [CAHOO-sah lee-MEH-nah]

Potato, avocado, tuna and hard-boiled egg in layers

This delicious and versatile potato dish is great for spring and summer outdoor events. Bring it to a picnic or to the beach. Try making filling variations, including using chicken, shrimp, or smoked salmon, and you'll go from a side dish to a full meal.

INGREDIENTS

2 pounds potatoes, peeled and roughly chopped

¼ cup olive oil

¼ cup fresh lime juice

Salt and pepper, to taste

½ cup mayonnaise

2 cans tuna

2 hard-boiled eggs, sliced into rounds

1 red onion, diced

2 avocados, peeled and sliced, for garnish

Black olives, for garnish

DIRECTIONS

1. Place the potatoes in a large pot with cool water and salt. Bring to boil and cook until potatoes are soft. Drain.

2. Mash the potatoes with a potato masher. Stir in olive oil, lime juice, and salt and pepper.

3. Line a casserole dish with plastic wrap. Spread half of the potato mash across the bottom. Spread mayonnaise all over the mashed potatoes, then spread the tuna over the mayonnaise, then onion over the tuna and hard boiled eggs over the onion, in layers.

4. Cover the filling with the remaining potato mash. Press lightly and cover with plastic wrap. Refrigerate for at least 3 hours.

5. Remove the plastic wrap from the top before inverting the casserole. Press a serving plate to the top of the casseole. Flip over and onto the plate. Remove the plastic wrap and spread with remaining mayonnaise. Garnish with avocado slices and black olives. Serve cool.

TIP

The selection of the casserole dish is important as this creates the outer shape of the layered dish. Use 3" round glasses to make pre-portioned personal-sized servings.

TOTAL TIME:
1 HOUR
DIFFICULTY:
EASY
PORTIONS:
6 SERVINGS

LOMO SALTEADO   [LOH-moh sahl-TEHAH-doh]

Stir-fry beef with soy sauce and fried potatoes

This popular Chinese and Peruvian fusion beef stir-fry boasts a combination of flavors and textures.

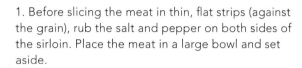

INGREDIENTS

2 pounds sirloin, cut into strips

2-3 tbsp. vegetable oil

2 garlic cloves, finely chopped

1 red onion, sliced into strips

1 white onion, sliced into strips

1 scallion, finely chopped

3 tomatoes, sliced into strips

1 yellow chili pepper (Peruvian aji Amarillo) sliced

1 tsp. ground cumin

3 tbsp. soy sauce

2 tbsp. wine vinegar

½ tsp. salt

½ tsp. pepper

½ fresh lime

Parsley, chopped for garnish

1½ cups French fried potatoes, to serve with the above

DIRECTIONS

1. Before slicing the meat in thin, flat strips (against the grain), rub the salt and pepper on both sides of the sirloin. Place the meat in a large bowl and set aside.

2. In a medium bowl, put in the onions, garlic, yellow chili pepper, tomatoes, and scallion; set aside.

3. Place a wok over high heat, heat the oil and stir in the meat, sear for about 2 or 3 minutes on both sides.

4. Remove the meat from the wok and set aside on a platter. In the same wok, add more vegetable oil if needed, stir in onions (red and white), then garlic, tomatoes and yellow chili and scallion, sauté for about 3 or 4 minutes or until onions are soft. Add soy sauce, wine vinegar, and cumin. Add back the reserved meat, add salt and pepper, squeeze the fresh lime over everything. Add French fries to the top and garnish with chopped parsley; serve immediately over white rice.

TIP

Asian influences are evident in the use of a wok to quickly fry the beef. If one is not available, use a fry pan with high sides to create a hot environment inside.

TOTAL TIME:
1 HOUR
DIFFICULTY:
EASY
PORTIONS:
6 SERVINGS

ANTICUCHOS   [ahn-tee-KOO-chohs]

Skewers of grilled marinated meat

This recipe is a special addition for any BBQ party. You can prepare this recipe with regular beef, chicken, or fish, but the traditional recipe calls for it to be made with beef heart.

INGREDIENTS

¼	cup wine vinegar
3	tbsp. vegetable oil
1	tbsp. parsley, finely chopped
1	tsp. hot paprika
1	tsp. ground aji amarillo (yellow aji)
1	tsp. ground turmeric
½	tsp. ground cumin
½	tsp. pepper
½	tsp. salt
2	pounds fresh beef heart, cut into ½ inch pieces, or any piece of meat that can be skewered

DIRECTIONS

1. In a large bowl, combine all ingredients except beef heart, or your choice of meat. Toss well. Add the heart and marinate for 30-45 minutes. While the heart marinates, heat the grill.

2. Now, thread 3 or 4 pieces of heart onto each skewer. When the grill is hot, place the anticuchos on the grill and brush with extra vegetable oil if necessary.

3. Grill the anticuchos until golden brown, about 4 minutes per side. Serve hot, just off the grill, and still on the skewer.

TIP

Have all of the other parts of your meal plated and served, since these cook up before you can say "Anticuchos anyone?"

TOTAL TIME:
1 HOUR
DIFFICULTY:
EASY
PORTIONS:
6 SERVINGS

LÚCUMA   [LU-Koo-Meh]

Lúcuma fruit smoothie

Peruvians love the flavor of lúcuma, a tropical fruit native to the Andean valley and available in the United States in Latin American grocery stores.

INGREDIENTS

3 lúcuma fruit, peeled

1 cup freshly squeezed orange juice

1 cup sugar

½ cup water

4 egg whites, at room temperature

1 cup whipping cream, very cool

   Mint leaves, for garnish

DIRECTIONS

1. In a blender mix lúcuma with orange juice. Set aside.

2. In a pan over medium-high heat, combine sugar and water and bring to boil to create a caramel.

3. Meanwhile, beat egg whites in a stand mixer until soft peaks form. Add caramel very slowly to the mixer and continue mixing. Add lúcuma puree, pouring small amounts as it's blending. Next, add whipping cream by hand very slowly as well.

4. Place in individual glasses and refrigerate at least 4 hours. Garnish with mint leaves just before serving.

TIP

This natural native fruit creates a delicious and richly filling drink that complements any meal.

TOTAL TIME:
5 HOURS
DIFFICULTY:
INTERMEDIATE
PORTIONS:
4 SERVINGS

PUERTO RICO

From 1898, when Puerto Rico became a possession of the United States, Americans have been fascinated by this Caribbean island in the Greater Antilles. It was called by early visitors "the land of perpetual June." The flowers, trees, fruits, and vegetables growing year-round astounded those who had previously experienced four separate seasons.

Though about one-twelfth the size of Cuba, Puerto Rico's geography is amazingly diverse. Long expanses of white shoreline are broken by tall, rocky bluffs. Fertile mountains give way to rich pastures, all fed by a multitude of rivers, springs, and waterfalls.

Corn is less abundant here than in other Latin American nations due to the hurricanes that easily uproot the stalks. Instead, tubers and low-growing vegetables like yams, beets, cassava, cantaloupes, and watermelon thrive.

The cuisine of Puerto Rico maintains aspects of all of its inhabitants: the early Tainos, the conquering Spanish, Africans, and of course Americans with whom its residents became fellow citizens in 1916. The food is highly seasoned and many dishes incorporate the aji caballero—a hot pepper unique to Puerto Rico.

Pork is the favored meat, with chicken second choice. Arroz con gandules, slow-roasted pork served with rice and pigeon peas, is both the national dish and a holiday tradition. Like many Puerto Rican recipes, its depth of flavor relies greatly on the sofrito used to season it. While each family's is a bit different, the key ingredients in this sautéed mélange are tomatoes, onions, fresh garlic, cilantro, and a variety of peppers. Sometimes bacon (which, like turkey, is an American import) or cured ham are diced into the blend.

While not a mainstay, seafood is an ingredient in several popular dishes. Asopao is a gumbo-like stew with rice and other meats. Mofongo, made with fried plantains and pork cracklings, is often topped with shrimp and garlic sauce.

Many Puerto Rican beverages are Caribbean inspired. Fresh tropical fruits like guava, mango, starfruit, and bananas are blended in myriad ways. The now multi-national piña colada was first served in a San Juan hotel bar in 1954. And, be it breakfast, lunch, or dinner, coffee and chocolate are present at nearly every meal.

Desserts like tres leches (three milk) cake and sweet potato balls add the perfect finishing touch.

Fortunately for mainlanders, most grocery stores stock all of the vegetables and condiments used in the following recipes. Take your taste buds on a trip to the West Indies without ever leaving your dining room.

MOJO ISLEÑO [MOH-hoh eehs-LEH-nyoh]

Puerto Rican sauce

This simple, yummy garlic sauce goes especially well with tostones (below) but makes a great accompaniment to grilled chicken, fish and meat.

INGREDIENTS

6-8	garlic cloves
¼	cup freshly squeezed lime juice
1	tbsp. freshly squeezed orange juice
1	tbsp. white vinegar
½	cup olive oil
½	tsp. salt
¼	tsp. oregano
2	tbsp. fresh cilantro
1	tbsp. fresh parsley
¼	tsp. paprika (optional)
¼	tsp. cumin (optional)

DIRECTIONS

Place all ingredients into a blender and blend 1-2 minutes or until smooth. Adjust salt and lime juice if it is necessary to taste. Store in refrigerator until used.

TOSTONES [Toast-HO-nehs]

Fried plantains

Use only green plantains to make these tostones, or twice-fried plantains - which are especially delicious when served with mojo sauce.

INGREDIENTS

2	green plantains
½	cup vegetable oil
	Salt to taste

DIRECTIONS

1. Peel plantains and cut into 1- to 1 1/4-inch thick slices.

2. Heat the oil in a large frying pan. Place the plantains in batches and fry until golden brown, about 2-3 minutes per side. Remove the plantains from pan and drain on paper towel.

3. Flatten the plantains using a press or a glass to flatten each slice to about 1/3 inch.

4. Return the slices to the hot oil and fry again until crispy. Season with salt and serve with mojo sauce.

TOTAL TIME:
15 MINUTES
DIFFICULTY:
EASY
PORTIONS:
1 CUP

TOTAL TIME:
25 MINUTES
DIFFICULTY:
EASY
PORTIONS:
4-6 SERVINGS

JUEYES HERVIDOS [HUEH-yehs ehr-VEEH-dohs]

Crab stew

Crab stew is very popular in Puerto Rican culture. Add some jarred sofrito sauce to the stew to punch it up a notch.

INGREDIENTS

1   tbsp. olive oil

1   onion, finely chopped

½   bell green pepper, finely chopped

½   bell red pepper, finely chopped

4   garlic cloves, finely chopped

4   tomatoes, chopped

2   tbsp. tomato paste

½   cup shrimp broth

½   tsp. oregano

½   tsp. cumin

Salt and pepper, to taste

1   pound lump crab meat or land crab with shells, thoroughly washed

½   cup white wine

1   tbsp. fresh cilantro, chopped

DIRECTIONS

1. In a large skillet, heat the olive oil, then sauté the onion, garlic, and green and red peppers until tender, about 5-7 minutes.

2. Add chopped tomato and tomato paste and toss well. Next, add shrimp broth, oregano, cumin, salt, pepper, and bring to a boil. Turn down heat to low and simmer for 5-8 minutes.

3. Add crabs and white wine and simmer for about 20-30 minutes. Sprinkle with fresh cilantro and serve with white rice.

TIP

Crab can be fresh or frozen, and if you don't have any crab-in-shells, you can shred the crabmeat throughout the soup.

TOTAL TIME:
1 HOUR
DIFFICULTY:
INTERMEDIATE
PORTIONS:
6 SERVINGS

LECHÓN ASADO   [leh-CHOHN ah-SAH-doh]

Roast pork

Puerto Rican roasted pork is delicious and moist and a remarkable recipe to share with family and friends on holidays and special occasions.

INGREDIENTS

- 8   pounds pork shoulder
- 10 garlic cloves, minced
- 1   tsp. oregano
- 1   tsp. cumin
- 4   tsp. salt
- 1   tsp. pepper
- 4   tbsp. olive oil
- 1   tbsp. freshly squeezed lime juice
- 2   tbsp. plus ¼ cup freshly squeezed orange juice

DIRECTIONS

1. With a sharp knife, make 3 to 4 individual 1-inch deep cuts into each side of the pork shoulder so that all of the flavors from the marinate mixture can infuse the meat and set aside on a board.

2. Using a mortar with pestle, crush together garlic, oregano, cumin, salt and pepper. Add olive oil, lime juice, and orange juice and mix well. Use your hands or a large spoon to spread this mixture all over the pork shoulder, adding some inside the small cuts.

3. Place the pork on a roasting pan, fat side up. Wrap the roast in plastic wrap and marinate overnight. (If you have time, it is much better to marinate 2 days before roasting.)

4. When you are ready to cook the meat, preheat oven to 325° F. Unwrap the pork, then tent with aluminum foil and place in the oven. Roast meat approximately 4 hours—or 40 minutes per pound.

5. After the first 3 hours, remove the aluminum foil tent and pour 1/4 cup freshly squeezed orange juice over the pork. Roast an additional hour uncovered, until the roast is cooked.

TIP

Classic and succulent, serve with rice and beans and garnish with fresh lime slices.

TOTAL TIME:
4 HOURS
(plus marinating time)
DIFFICULTY:
INTERMEDIATE
PORTIONS:
8-10 SERVINGS

POLLO AL JEREZ   [POH-yoh Ahl heh-REHS]

Chicken in sherry

Chicken in sherry is a favorite traditional Puerto Rican dish. You can add 2-3 fresh tomatoes, quartered, to the mix to give the dish another dimension.

INGREDIENTS

	Salt and pepper
1	tsp. thyme
2-3	pounds chicken pieces (legs, breast) or the whole chicken cut in large pieces
1	small onion, sliced
2	garlic cloves, finely chopped
2	scallions, sliced
4	potatoes, quartered
½	cup chicken broth
3	bay leaves
1	tbsp. olive oil
1	cup sherry
¼	cup parsley, finely chopped

DIRECTIONS

1. Season the chicken with salt and pepper and sprinkle with thyme.

2. Heat olive oil in a large skillet over high heat. Add chicken pieces and sear on all sides. Remove chicken from pan and set aside.

3. In the same pan, sauté onion, garlic, and scallions until soft, about 5-7 minutes.

4. Add the chicken back to the skillet, along with the potatoes, chicken broth, and bay leaves. Cover and let simmer for 30 minutes.

5. Add sherry to the pan. Cover and simmer for 10 minutes more.

6. Sprinkle parsley over chicken and serve warm.

TIP

Cut the meat from the bone and make sandwiches with any left-overs that might remain.

TOTAL TIME:
1 HOUR
DIFFICULTY:
INTERMEDIATE
PORTIONS:
6 SERVINGS

NISPEROS DE BATATA [NHEES-peh-rohs deh bah-TAH-tah]

Sweet potato balls with coconut, cloves and cinnamon

These sweet potato balls have an exquisite Caribbean aroma and a rich flavor. To make them even quicker, consider cooking the sweet potatoes in advance.

INGREDIENTS

3   sweet potatoes, peeled and cut into chunks

1   cup coconut milk

1   cup shredded coconut

1½ cup brown sugar

3   egg yolks

1   tsp. vanilla

1-2 tsp. ground cinnamon

Whole cloves, for garnish

DIRECTIONS

1. In a large pot, boil sweet potatoes until tender, about 20-25 minutes. Mash and set aside.

2. Add coconut milk, shredded coconut, sugar, egg yolks, and vanilla to a pot and bring to boil over medium-high heat.

3. Reduce heat to medium and add sweet potato mash. Mix well with a wooden spoon until the mixture separates completely from bottom and sides of pan. Remove from heat and cool completely.

4. When cool, shape mixture into small balls. Dust with ground cinnamon and garnish with whole cloves.

ARROZ CON LECHE [ah-RROHS KOHN LEH-cheh]

Rice pudding

Rum provides the authentic Puerto Rican flavor to this simple dessert. It can be served warm or cool. This recipe is perfect for holidays.

INGREDIENTS

½   cup white rice (washed)

3   cups whole milk

1   cup sugar

4   cinnamon sticks

3   whole cloves

½   tsp. fresh lemon zest

1   egg

1   tsp. vanilla extract

1   cup raisins (soak with the rum)

½   cup dark rum

DIRECTIONS

1. Bring the following ingredients to a boil over medium heat: milk, rice, cinnamon sticks, cloves and lemon zest. When the milk starts boiling, reduce the heat to low and let simmer until rice is soft and milk has reduced, about 30 to 40 minutes, stirring occasionally. Add sugar and let simmer for 5 to 10 minutes more.

2. Whisk the egg until thickened. Pour into the rice mixture and stir until combined thoroughly. Remove from the heat and add soaked raisins and pour into a serving bowl or individual serving cups. Dash with cinnamon powder and let cool before refrigerating. Serve cool or warm.

TOTAL TIME:
1 HOUR
DIFFICULTY:
EASY
PORTIONS:
25 BALLS

TOTAL TIME:
1½ HOURS
DIFFICULTY:
MEDIUM
PORTIONS:
6 SERVINGS

VENEZUELA

Venezuela's hottest cities sit along the north-western Caribbean coast where temperatures average 100 degrees or more. Tropical fruit drinks are important and enjoyable components of the daily diet. Arepa – a daily bread – is one of the most popular dishes in Venezuela and is often split open and filled with cheese and meat. Venezuelan cuisine has a lot of European influences such as Italian, French and Spanish. Indigenous and African influences are also present and help in making Venezuela a very diverse country.

Each region has its own particular food; on the coast, a rich variety of seafood is easily found. In the Andean region, food is well known for cured meats, sausages and fresh trout. In the Amazon region, vegetables such as yucca, corn, beans, and bananas, among others, are very popular.

In extreme contrast to the heat of the coasts and central region are the Venezuelan Mountains. High points such as Pico Bolivar and Pico Humboldt are glacial regions with year-round, sub-zero temperatures. Falling between these two contradictory climates are the Guiana Highlands, where daytime temperatures average 70 degrees.

Like most of its Latin American neighbors, Venezuela's staples are corn, rice, plantains, beans, and fruits like the soft, pulpy guanabana. Unlike in most of the United States, however, fresh produce is always in season. Plantains, the national staple, are served with most meals as well as in soups and stews.

Holiday cooking in Venezuela is a family affair, although, as with most Christmas meals, no two families prepare them the same way. Hallaca, a mixture of cornmeal, beef, pork, olives and raisins cooked like a stew, is the traditional holiday dish, though flavors and recipes are specific to each region. These ingredients are tied inside banana leaves and steamed. Because so much time is required in the preparation, households cook a quantity sufficient to last the season.

Other popular corn-based dishes include cachapas, which resemble pancakes folded around fresh cheese, and tequenos, spiral-shaped dough stuffed with cheese and deep fried.

Plantains are cooked a myriad of ways. One snack known as tostones uses green plantains. Slices are fried, pulled from the grease, pounded flat and sprinkled with salt. They are served and enjoyed much like our potato chips.

As with other South American countries, immigrants have strongly impacted the cuisine of Venezuela. Italian cookery is particularly influential. Ensalada caprese is a simple yet exceedingly flavorful salad composed of tomato slices, mozzarella slices, and fresh basil leaves. Pasticho is the Venezuelan take on lasagne.

Bien me sabe is Venezuela's favored dessert. This liquor-drenched sponge cake is iced with rich coconut cream. The name translates to "tastes good to me"– likely the same thing you'll say about each of the following Venezuelan recipes.

CACHAPAS   [Kah-CHA-Pahs]

Thick pancake-like corn cakes

These Venezuelan fresh corn pancakes can be served at any meal with cheese or pork. For a sweeter taste, use whole sweet corn.

INGREDIENTS

- 2 cups fresh or frozen corn kernels
- ¼ cup buttermilk
- 2 tbsp. cornmeal
- 1 tsp. sugar
- ½ tsp. salt
- ¼ tsp. pepper
- 2 eggs
- 2 tbsp. butter
- 1 cup mozzarella cheese, grated

DIRECTIONS

1. In a blender, combine corn with buttermilk, corn-meal, sugar, salt, and pepper. When combined, add eggs and 1 tbsp. of the melted butter.

2. Heat a large pan over medium low heat. Add the remaining tbsp. of butter. When butter is melted, spoon the batter into the pan, forming 2 to 3 inch-round discs. Cook 2-3 minutes each side.

3. Sprinkle mozzarella cheese on half of each disc, then fold over to create half-moon shapes. Heat until cheese is melted. Serve warm.

TIP

Cachapas are a traditional and versatile Venezuelan snack. It can also be served for breakfast with some fried pork or chorizo.

TOTAL TIME:
25 MINUTES
DIFFICULTY:
EASY
PORTIONS:
6 SERVINGS

PERICO [peh-REE-koh]

Scrambled eggs with onion, tomato, and pepper

Venezuelan scrambled eggs are very colorful and tasty! For more color, add some sweet peas or other vegetables when you add in the tomatoes.

INGREDIENTS

4-6 eggs

2 tbsp. milk

1 tsp. vegetable oil

1 tbsp. butter

1 onion, finely chopped

½ leek, finely chopped

2 garlic cloves, finely chopped

½ green bell pepper, finely chopped

1 tomato, finely chopped

Salt and pepper, to taste

1 tbsp. cilantro leaves

DIRECTIONS

1. Lightly whisk eggs and milk together and set aside.

2. Heat a frying pan over medium heat. Add oil and butter. When butter is melted, add the onion, leek, garlic, and bell pepper, and sauté. When the onions are tender and translucent add tomato.

3. Cover and reduce heat. Simmer for 3-4 minutes.

4. Gently fold in eggs. Seasoned with salt and pepper and cook uncovered for 3-4 minutes. Serve immediately with arepa (p. 152) on the side. Garnish with cilantro leaves.

TIP

Satisfying and rich due to the inclusion of onion, leek, and garlic, this classic breakfast pleases everyone.

TOTAL TIME:
20 MINUTES
DIFFICULTY:
EASY
PORTIONS:
4 SERVINGS

AREPAS   [ah-REH-pahs]

Griddle-fried corn cakes made from masarepa

Arepa is like daily bread in Venezuela. They are most fun when you make a party of creating them - prepare a variety of fillings and invite family and friends to share in the fun!

INGREDIENTS

- 2   cups masarepa
- 2   cups warm water
- 2   tbsp. melted butter
- 1   tsp. salt
-      Pinch of sugar
-      Vegetable oil

- 1   cup shredded cheese
- 1   cup cooked chicken, shredded
- 1   cup cooked meat (pork or beef), shredded
- 1   stick butter

DIRECTIONS

1. In a large bowl dissolve salt and sugar in the warm water. Stir in melted butter. Then, little by little, add corn flour and work with hands until shortening is completely incorporated. To avoid lumps, work quickly with hands until dough is uniform. Keep dough covered with damp kitchen towel and set aside for about 10-15 minutes. Dough should be moist and easy to handle.

2. Preheat oven at 350° F. Shape dough into balls and flatten into discs about 4 inches in diameter and 2 inches thick. If dough starts cracking, add more liquid. Also, keep hands wet to make the dough easier to handle.

3. Coat the bottom of a large fry pan with vegetable oil and heat over medium high heat. Cook arepas until golden brown on both sides - about 2-3 minutes per side.

4. Place the arepas directly onto the oven racks. Bake for 8-10 minutes or until they puff up.

5. Split each arepa and fill with cheese, shredded chicken, or meat, and a pat of butter. Serve warm.

TIP

Venezuelan arepas can be grilled, baked or fried, cut lengthwise and stuffed with fillings ranging from the classic ham and cheese to the more complex, including shredded beef. The prevalence of the stuffed bread is relatively new, dating back only to 1950. Prior to that, it was consumed as a bread, not a sandwich.

TOTAL TIME:
45 MINUTES
DIFFICULTY:
INTERMEDIATE
PORTIONS:
8 SERVINGS

BOLLO PICANTE VEGETARIANO [BOH-yoh pee-KAHN-teh beh-heh-tah-reeAH-noh]

Steamed spicy vegetarian cornmeal roll

Bollos are traditionally made by using whatever is leftover from making hallacas, the traditional Christmas dish in Venezuela. The process of making bollos is much simpler because the ingredients are incorporated into the dough. This is a vegetarian version of bollos.

INGREDIENTS

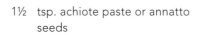

- 2 tbsp. olive oil
- 1 small onion, minced
- ½ green pepper, minced
- 1 tsp. chili flakes
- ½ cup vegetable oil
- 1½ tsp. achiote paste or annatto seeds
- 1 cup masarepa (corn flour)
- 1½ cups warm water
- 1 tsp. salt
- 1 potato, cooked and mashed
- 1 tbsp. capers, chopped
- 2 tbsp. pimiento-stuffed green olives, chopped
- 4 banana leaves about 8-inches long each

DIRECTIONS

1. In a skillet, heat olive oil. Add onion, green pepper, and chili flakes and sautee until onion is soft, about 5-7 minutes.

2. In a small pot, heat vegetable oil over low heat. Add achiote paste or annatto seeds. Heat until the oil takes on the color. Remove from heat.

3. Combine the masarepa, warm water, and salt in a medium bowl. Add mashed potato and mix into a dough.

4. Add 4 tbsp vegetable oil mixture to the masarepa mixture, reserving the rest to brush the banana leaves. Combine well. Next fold in the onion mixture, capers, and olives.

5. Brush banana leaves with the remaining vegetable oil mixture. Divide the dough into 4 equal portions and spread each of the banana leaves with one of the quarters of the dough. On each, fold the leaves over the dough and then fold down the sides. Tie each bollo twice with baker's twine.

6. In a large pot, boil 3 quarts of water. Arrange the bollos in the boiling water and set the heat to low. Cook for about 15 minutes. Serve warm.

TIP

You can use baker's twine for tying the bollos, if that's not handy, use a cotton yarn.

TOTAL TIME:
25 MINUTES
DIFFICULTY:
EASY
PORTIONS:
4 SERVINGS

PASTEL DE CHUCHO [pahs-TEHL deh CHOO-choh]

Fish lasagna

This sweet and salty dish has a Caribbean influence. It is typically made in Venezuela with a salty fish called "choco."

INGREDIENTS

- 1 tbsp. olive oil
- 1 onion, finely chopped
- 3 green onions (scallions), finely chopped
- 6 garlic cloves, finely chopped
- ½ green bell pepper, finely chopped
- ½ red bell pepper, finely chopped
- 1 leek, finely chopped
- 2 tomatoes, roughly chopped
- 1 tsp. ground cumin
- ½ tsp. ground oregano
- ½ tsp. salt
- ½ tsp. pepper
- 2 cans tuna in water, drained
- ½ cup olives, chopped
- ¼ cup capers, chopped
- 4 eggs, lightly beaten
- ½ cup seasoned breadcrumbs
- 3 potatoes, peeled, cooked, sliced
- 6 ripe plantains, sliced and fried
- 2 cups cheddar cheese, shredded

DIRECTIONS

1. Heat oil in a skillet over medium heat. Add the onions, garlic, peppers, and leek, and sauté until tender, about 5-7 minutes. Stir in tomato, then season with cumin, oregano, salt, and pepper.

2. Reduce the heat and simmer for 3-4 minutes. Then stir in tuna, olives, and capers. Remove from heat and set aside.

3. Lightly beat eggs. Add breadcrumbs to beaten eggs and mix to form a batter.

4. Preheat the oven at 300° F. Lightly grease a glass baking dish.

5. Now assemble the lasagna. Add one layer of potato, one layer of plantain, one layer of fish mixture, half egg mixture, then the cheese. Repeat and finish with cheese.

6. Bake uncovered for 30 minutes. Serve immediately.

TIP

Queso blanco can be substituted for cheddar cheese if it is available.

TOTAL TIME:
1 HOUR
DIFFICULTY:
INTERMEDIATE
PORTIONS:
6 SERVINGS

PONCHE CREMA   [POHN-cheh KREH-mah]

Egg nog

Everybody has their own family recipe for Christmas egg nog. Adjust the amount of rum and brandy to your taste.

INGREDIENTS

1   14-ounce can sweetened condensed milk

1   cup milk

1   cup coconut milk

2   cinnamon sticks

2   whole cloves

    Pinch of salt

4   egg yolks, lightly beaten

¼   cup rum

2   tbsp. brandy

    Ground nutmeg, to garnish

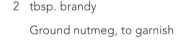

DIRECTIONS

1. Pour the milks into a medium pot over medium high-heat. Add cinnamon sticks, cloves, and salt.

2. As the milk heats, stir constantly with a wooden spoon. When it begins to boil, remove from heat. Slowly stir in egg yolks then return to stove, stirring constantly on low heat for an additional 2 minutes.

3. Remove from stove and cool. Add the mixture to a blender and blend until smooth. Strain.

4. Add rum and brandy and combine well. Bottle and refrigerate for about 2 hours. When cool, serve in glasses and garnish with nutmeg.

TIP

The combination of both rum and brandy makes this favorite holiday egg nog specific to Venezuela.

TOTAL TIME:
2½ HOURS
DIFFICULTY:
EASY
PORTIONS:
4 SERVINGS

BESITOS DE COCO   [beh-SEE-tohs deh KOH-koh]

Coconut "kisses"

For a more natural coconut taste in these delicious Venezuelan coconut cookies, use fresh shredded coconut.

INGREDIENTS

2¼   cups fresh shredded coconut
     or unsweetened shredded
     coconut

3   eggs yolks, lightly beaten

1   cup brown sugar

2   tbsp. butter

½   tsp. cinnamon

½   tsp. allspice

½   tsp. lemon zest

1   tsp. vanilla extract

½   cup flour

DIRECTIONS

1. Preheat oven at 350° F. Line a cookie sheet with parchment paper and set aside.

2. In a large bowl, mix 2 cups coconut with egg yolks and vanilla. Blend well with a wooden spoon, then add brown sugar, butter, cinnamon, allspice, lemon zest, and flour. Work into a dough.

3. Form the dough into balls and place over lined cookie sheet. Bake for 20 minutes or until golden brown. Remove from sheet and sprinkle with remaining coconut. Cool on a rack.

TIP

Light, crunchy and easy to prepare, these make a huge impression without a lot of fuss in the kitchen.

APPENDIX

METRIC CONVERSIONS

(Conversions are approximate)

IMPERIAL	METRIC
¼ teaspoon	1 ml
½ teaspoon	2 ml
1 teaspoon	5 ml
1 tablespoon	15 ml
2 tablespoons	25 ml
3 tablespoons	50 ml
¼ cup	50 ml
1/3 cup	75 ml
½ cup	125 ml
2/3 cup	150 ml
¾ cup	175 ml
1 cup	250 ml

YIELDS FOR COMMON INGREDIENTS

(Yields are approximate)

INGREDIENT	THE RECIPE CALLS FOR:	YOU WILL NEED:
Butter	1 cup	2 sticks
Cheese, shredded	1 cup	4 ounces
Flour, all purpose	3 ½ cups	1 pound
Honey	1 cup	12 ounces
Raisins	1 cup	5 ounces
Sugar, granulated	2 cups	1 pound
Sugar, powdered	4 cups	1 pound

INDEX

PHOTO CREDITS